Designing for
HUMANITY

Award-Winning Designs Meeting People's Changing Needs

Designing for
HUMANITY

Award-Winning Designs Meeting People's Changing Needs

by the Industrial Designers Society of America

The Library of Applied Design

An Imprint of
PBC International, Inc.

New York

Distributor to the book trade in the United States and Canada:

Rizzoli International Publications Inc.
300 Park Avenue South
New York, NY 10010

Distributor to the art trade in the United States:

PBC International, Inc.
One School Street
Glen Cove, NY 11542
1-800-527-2826
Fax 516-676-2738

Distributor to the art trade in Canada:

Letraset Canada, Ltd.
170 Duffield Drive
Markham, Ontario L6G 1B5, Canada

Distributed throughout the rest of the world by:

Hearst Books International
1350 Avenue of the Americas
New York, NY 10019

Library of Congress Cataloging-in-Publication
Data
Designing for humanity : award-winning designs
    meeting people's changing needs / [compiled]
    by the Industrial Designers Society of
    America.
        p.   cm.
    Includes index.
    1. Design, Industrial.   I. Industrial
    Designers Society of America.
    TS171.D48   1991
    745.2--dc20   91-12638
    ISBN   0-86636-140-5   CIP

*CAVEAT—Information in this text is believed ac-
curate, and will pose no problem for the student
or casual reader. However, the author was often
constrained by information contained in signed re-
lease forms, information that could have been in
error or not included at all. Any misinformation
(or lack of information) is the result of failure in
these attestations. The author has done whatever
is possible to insure accuracy.*

Color separation, printing and binding by
Toppan Printing Co. (H.K.) Ltd. Hong Kong

Typography by
TypeLink, Inc.

10 9 8 7 6 5 4 3 2 1

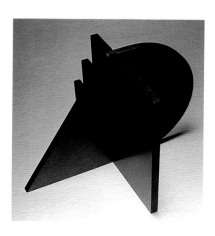

The Industrial Design Excellence Award

1988 IDEA Jury

Chair:
Charles Pelly, IDSA
Designworks/USA

James Ryan, IDSA
Henry Dreyfuss Associates

Jack Beduhn, IDSA
NCR Corp.

Loyd Moore, IDSA
Technology Design

David Tompkins, FIDSA
HIMONT

Jack Kelly, IDSA
Studio 222 Kelley Group Inc.

1989 IDEA Jury

Chair: *Jack Beduhn, IDSA*
NCR Corp.

Clyde Foles, IDSA
Center for Creative Studies

Brian Kane, IDSA
Kane Design Studio

Barbara Lewis, IDSA
Barbara K. Lewis Industrial Design

V. Lorenzo Porcelli, IDSA
Procellia Associates

Gianfranco Zaccai, IDSA
Design Continuum

1990 IDEA Jury

Chair: *Gianfranco Zaccai, IDSA*
Design Continuum

Peter Edward Lowe, IDSA
Interform

Bill Moggridge, IDSA
ID Two

Patricia Moore, IDSA
Moore & Associates

Louis Nelson, IDSA
Louis Nelson Associates Inc.

Martin Smith, IDSA
Art Center College of Design

Sandor Weisz, FIDSA
Dictaphone Corp.

CONTENTS

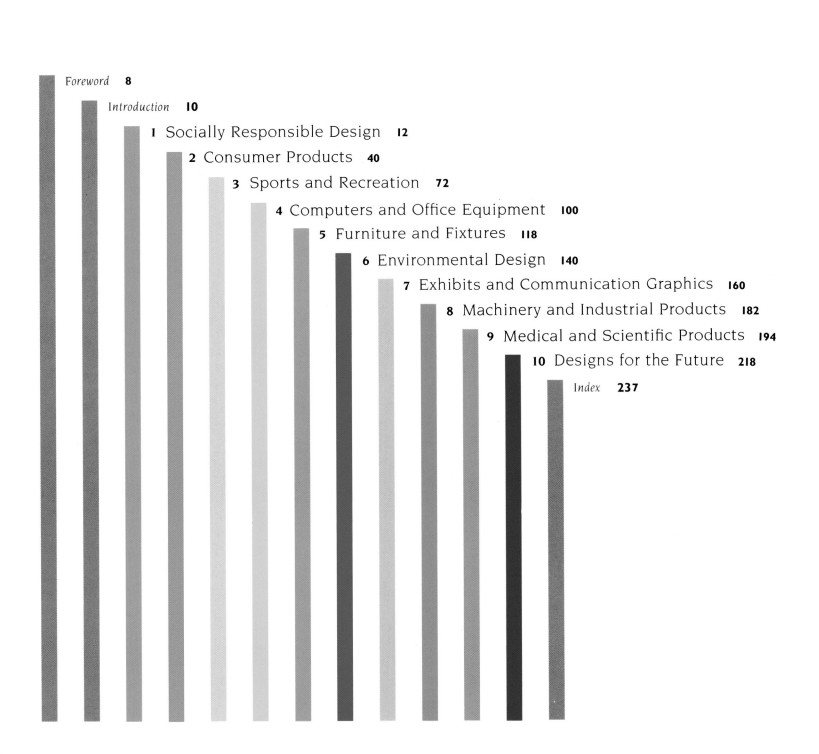

FOREWORD

Patricia A. Moore, IDSA, is principal of Moore & Associates in Phoenix, Arizona. An internationally renowned designer and gerontologist, she provides research and design in new products, environments, services and marketing strategies for consumers over the age of 50 and persons with special support needs. She holds undergraduate degrees in graphic design and industrial and environmental design from Rochester Institute of Technology, and two master's degrees—one in psychology and counseling, the other in human development.

From the moment that our Cro-Magnon ancestors chipped stones to create cutting tools, we have designed. Creating for our comfort, providing for our existence, responding to the daily challenges that impact our lives is a matter of design. The places and things that make up our individual realms are the results of someone's daring, thinking and action. Throughout history, designers have been those people who challenge the norm, rise to the occasion and seize the opportunity to make a difference for all lives.

It is a noble pursuit, the course of the designer. The curiosity of DaVinci made way for the flight of the Wright brothers. The first combustion engine led to rockets capable of launching us into space. The invention of the moment gives birth to the products of the future.

In this century, the design of things became known as the profession of "industrial design." The grandfathers of the field—Loewy, Teague, Dreyfuss—gave shape to the products that fill our lives. Automobiles, airplanes, telephones: all of the things which we, as consumers, have come to expect and require are made possible by the creativity of the art and science that is design.

By the 1960s, product designers found themselves faced by ever-growing challenges. The concerns of poverty, the environment and accessibility brought designers into a new role, as arbitrators of the quality of life. Determination of the shape and scope of our cities, protection and support of fragile resources that are our planet and the independence and autonomy of all persons, throughout the course of their life's entirety, catapulted the importance of good industrial design and the position of the industrial designer into a position of critical importance.

Just as DaVinci questioned the accepted, the designer of today must re-define what is known. Today's answers must support tomorrow's questions. There has never been a more exciting or vital time for the contribution of industrial design, and the need for "humanism" in industrial design has never been more critical. By focusing our talents on the needs of the individual, we have given birth to a new order: humanity by design. This philosophic order doesn't ask, "Why?" But rather, "Why not?" We don't speak of limitations. We create opportunities.

The emergence of "universality" in design supports the conviction that where there is a deficit, we will present a solution. Where there is ignorance, we will strive for enlightenment. Where there is a roadblock, we will create a pathway.

● No longer can we speak of the "*disabled*." Our charter is to enhance a person's abilities, with the recognition that we are all of us, merely "*differently*-abled" and design and industrial designers, the "enablers."

● Gone is the time when we focused on the variable of age as a limitation to response. Our "elders," not the "elderly," require the impact of good design in their lives, as do people of all ages. From birth to death, it is the life span that is the domain of the designer.

● No longer do we create packages and products that deplete resources and impact the environment without asking the question: "Have we considered the interconnectedness of it all?"

As we enter into the next millennium, the role of the industrial designer will be that of the navigator, the translator for what we want and wish, our hopes and our desires. There has never been a more crucial time for our work; never a greater opportunity for our impact. Beyond providing for a successful bottom line for the corporate realm, industrial design will perpetuate the presence of the companies which address our consumers needs.

Ours is an amazing charter. Beyond the confines of the aesthetic, we have the capacity to fashion the very quality of life itself. Design is no longer a mere variable in determining the course of the future, it is the very means of our survival.

The products featured in this volume are evidence of the *solution* that is industrial *design*. The items found in these pages are the result of the research, conceptualization and testing that is the world of industrial design. The quantum leap that has been achieved in this century gives rise to the debate about what will be in all of our tomorrows.

INTRODUCTION

Designing for humanity is the ideal to which industrial designers subscribe above all others. They enter the profession of industrial design motivated to improve the lot of humankind by better harnessing technology and better expressing it in form. Although some may find their efforts stymied and their ideals dulled in the course of their careers, rare indeed is the industrial designer who would not prefer to contribute to the benefit of people. Theirs is not the bottom-line impulse of the statistician, but the impulse of compassion and openness to the different contributions everyone can make, whatever their various limitations might be.

The world today needs this humane, compassionate professional to temper the struggle for competitive survival. No stranger to the demand for corporate returns on investment, the industrial designer's talent for innovation can and, given the opportunity, does address human needs while meeting corporate objectives. Indeed, time and again, industrial designers have improved corporate returns by insisting on considering people's needs. Thus, design for humanity is not a concept that refers only to design for people with disabilities or people who are aging. It means finding the best way to meet the needs of all people through a design.

For the past decade, the Industrial Designers Society of America (IDSA) has sponsored the Industrial Design Excellence Awards program (IDEA). One of its prime criteria of design excellence has been "benefit to the user." All the entrants have been forced to think about their design—be it an environment, exhibit, product or package—from the user's point of view. Time and again, the winners have been selected because they excelled in their service to the user.

These designs have organized complex functions more simply and intuitively in medical and scientific equipment. They have made products more comfortable to use and the information in exhibits more accessible to people with a range of physical abilities and educational backgrounds. They have overcome hazards and have even tried to make using the product more fun.

The projects shown in this book were selected for either Gold, Silver or Bronze awards in 1988, 1989 and 1990. They have been clustered, not by their IDEA category per se, but in broad groups that reflect either their industry or their primary character or benefits. Their descriptions focus on the user's benefit although most had other outstanding qualities as well. In fact, in order to be selected for recognition, the projects must have done very well in these other criteria: innovation; benefits to the client; customer appeal of the appearance; and appropriate use of materials and processes. Beginning in 1990, the designs also had to excel in positive social impact, a new criteria inspired by the need to more explicitly address industrial design's responsibility to humanity and the world as a whole.

Appropriately, this book begins by focusing on those designs that most explicitly address human needs. The chapter, "Socially Responsible Design," encompasses work that meets the needs of the disabled and handicapped. It also includes work whose environmental impact improves on past designs, and it includes projects that have met urgent health needs. The very fact that many of the projects shown in this chapter were selected before the "positive social impact" criterion was instituted demonstrates that the profession's commitment to this ideal is alive and well.

The winners shown in this book have been selected by juries made up of the most well-respected US industrial designers. Waiving the right to enter the competition in the year they served on the jury, the jurors contributed their insight and expertise to IDSA as volunteers, dedicated professionals prepared to help their profession find excellence and celebrate it.

IDSA is made up of more than 2,000 such volunteers and members, and has grown steadily since its formation in 1965. Its membership has doubled in the past decade alone as have the number of services it provides. These services include publication of a journal, newsletter, and annual directory; the conduct of a national conference and five district conferences; support to 25 active chapters; committees that address topics ranging from ethics and education to design management and environmental concerns; liaison on college/university accreditation; and federal lobbying for passage of better intellectual property protection for industrial design.

Last, but by no means least, IDSA has a strong press relations effort that has resulted in the avalanche of coverage and interest the profession is receiving today.

Much of that coverage has come in the *Wall Street Journal* and *Business Week*. In fact, *Business Week* has identified industrial design as a cutting-edge business issue and has chosen to sponsor the Industrial Design Excellence Awards program, beginning in 1991. In so doing, this magazine has recognized the integral role industrial design must play for corporations to compete successfully today. It is to the editors' credit that they understand that much of that benefit comes from industrial design's concern for user needs.

And so this book is appropriately named. Making the winners fit this focus was not a strain although not all the designs excelled primarily in user benefit. Industrial design's commitment to humanity might need more opportunity to reach full expression than it gets in today's business climate. But this book shows that, whenever possible, industrial designers do stand up for humanity and strive, often against considerable odds, to produce the best possible design.

CHAPTER 1

SOCIALLY RESPONSIBLE DESIGN

AVC ADVANTAGE VOTING MACHINE

"This machine captured the imagination of the IDEA jury with its refined, distinctive and consistent detailing."

—*Juror* **Sandor Weisz,** FIDSA

DRIVER ASSESSMENT SYSTEM

"It is an outstanding example of design professionals and the public sector joining forces to improve the quality of life for others."

—*Jury Chair* **Gianfranco Zaccai,** IDSA

INFANT CAR SEAT

"I am particularly impressed by the concept because it delivers a broad range of options and variations for use by parents and caregivers."

—*Juror* **Patricia Moore,** IDSA

CHILD STAIR RAIL

"This is one of those ideas that you say to yourself, 'why didn't I think of that!'"

—*Juror* **Martin Smith,** IDSA

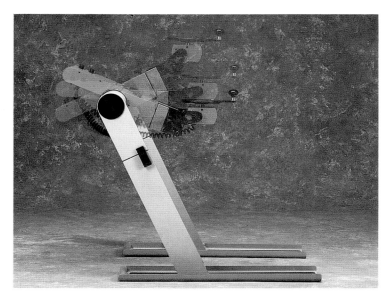

PRODUCT
Driver Assessment System
DESIGNERS
David Mehaffey, James Machen, Eddie
Machen, Edgar Montague
DESIGN FIRM
Machen Montague
CLIENT/MFR
State of North Carolina Department
of Human Resources
AWARD
Gold 1990

The portable, lightweight and
compact Driver Assessment
System (DAS), is used to de-
termine the exact specifica-
tions required for converting
an automobile for a disabled
driver and to test the individual's capacity to drive the
customized vehicle. Easily
transported to the disabled
person's home, the DAS
eliminates the need to
transport the person to a
testing site.

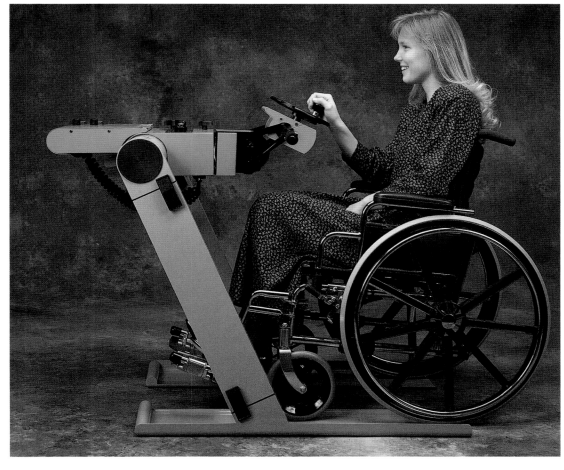

PRODUCT
Seattle LightFoot™
DESIGNER
David G. Firth, BSID
DESIGN FIRM
M + IND
CLIENT/MFR
M + IND
AWARD
Silver 1990

The Seattle LightFoot is a lightweight, modular, dynamic response prosthetic foot suitable for use by lower limb amputees of all ages and activity levels. This design reduces the weight of its predecessor by 33 percent. The LightFoot reduces energy consumption of the user, allowing increased activity levels with less exertion—a great value to all users, but particularly to geriatric patients.

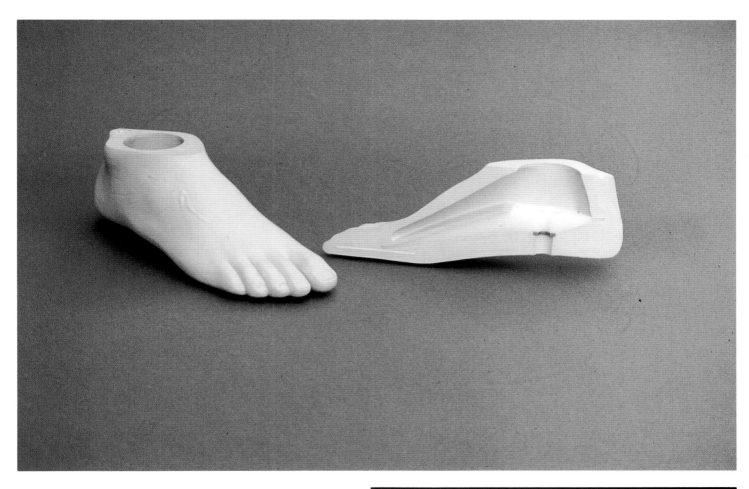

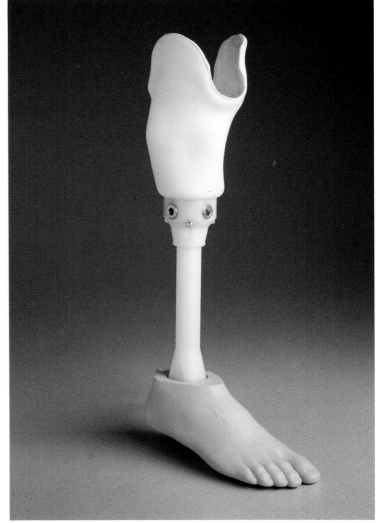

PRODUCT
Slingshot Wheelchair for Children
DESIGNER
Adele Linarducci while a student at
Rochester Institute of Technology
AWARD
Bronze 1990

The Slingshot is a wheelchair
sensitive to the physical and
psychological needs of children aged six to eleven who
want to gain strength and
dexterity by using a manual
rather than an electric wheelchair. The Slingshot feature
provides a gentle nudge,
solving the problem most
children encounter with
wheelchair operation—the
lack of sufficient physical
strength to set the chair in
motion.

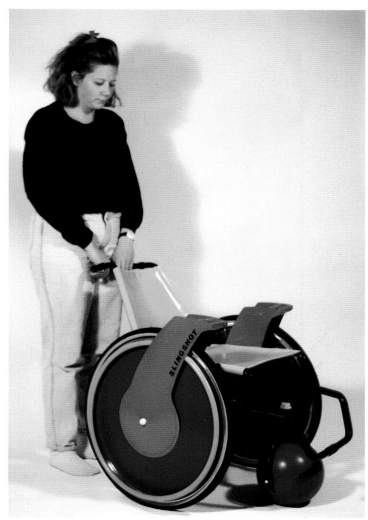

PRODUCT
Slingshot Wheelchair for Children
DESIGNER
Adele Linarducci while a student at
Rochester Institute of Technology
AWARD
Bronze 1990

The Slingshot is a wheelchair
sensitive to the physical and
psychological needs of children aged six to eleven who
want to gain strength and
dexterity by using a manual
rather than an electric wheelchair. The Slingshot feature
provides a gentle nudge,
solving the problem most
children encounter with
wheelchair operation—the
lack of sufficient physical
strength to set the chair in
motion.

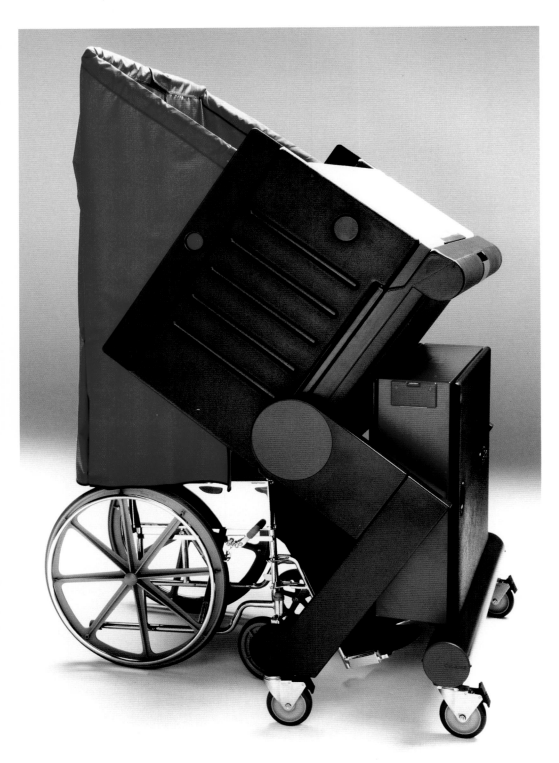

PRODUCT
AVC Advantage Electronic Voting Machine
DESIGNERS
James H. Bleck, Scott Wakefield, John Thrailkill
DESIGN FIRM
Bleck Design Group
CLIENT/MFR
Sequoia Pacific Systems Corp.
AWARD
Gold 1990

The AVC is designed for the needs of all voters, including the elderly and disabled. Voters require little instruction because of the design's simplicity and visual clues. The AVC provides election officials and voters with a secure, easy-to-operate and cost-effective voting system.

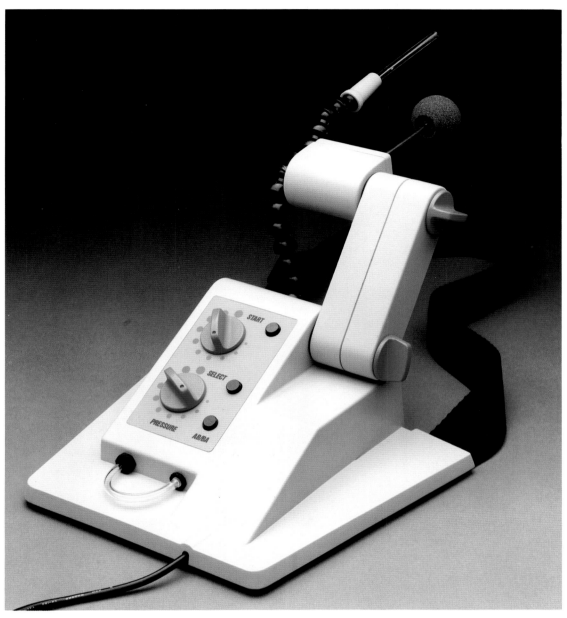

PRODUCT
Hands Free Controller for the
Nintendo Entertainment System
DESIGNERS
Lance Barr, John Cordell, Don James
DESIGN FIRM
Nintendo of America, Inc.
CLIENT/MFR
Nintendo of America, Inc.
AWARD
Silver 1989

The Hands Free Controller (HFC) is designed for individuals with limited hand or body mobility. Worn on the chest, it has a chin-activated joystick, as well as a "sip and puff" tube that activates the button functions found on typical controllers. HFC is designed to accommodate a wide variety of ages and physical types.

PRODUCT
PRM-1 Remote Control
DESIGNERS
Doug Patton, Rick Jung
DESIGN FIRM
Patton Design
CLIENT/MFR
Mitsubishi Electric
AWARD
Gold 1990

This remote control represents a solution based on the human need for simplicity. The PRM-1 provides the most minimal controls needed to watch TV. Focusing on the three critical controls, the PRM-1 is comfortable, easy to use, fun and simple. No written clues are needed to operate it because the design relies successfully on visual cues.

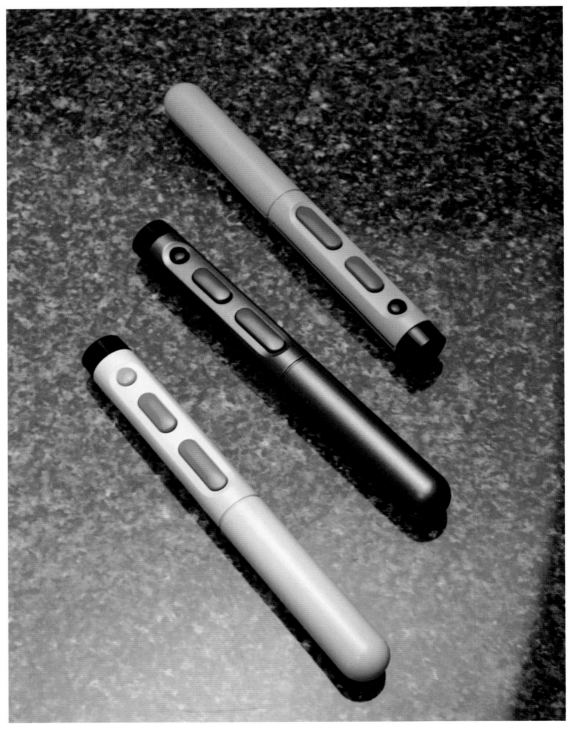

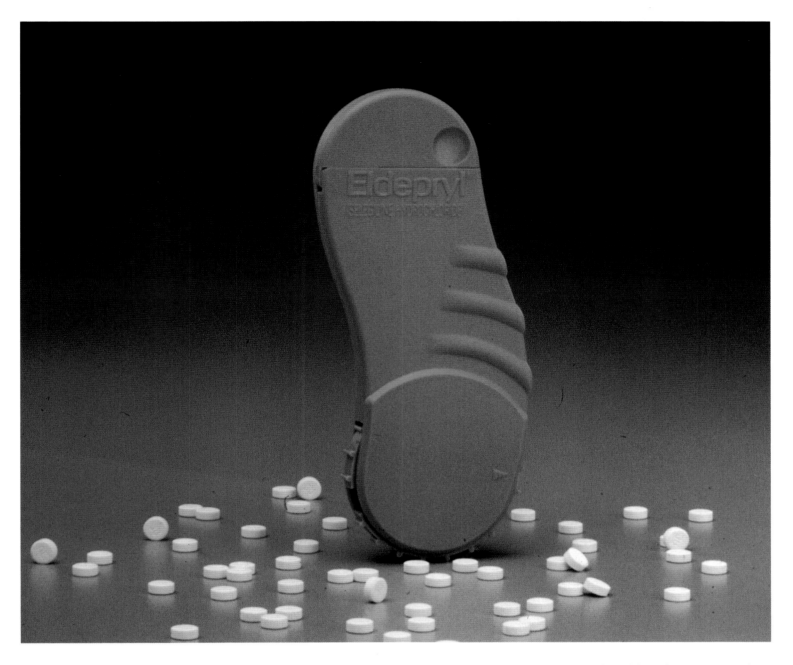

PRODUCT
Eldepryl Pill Dispenser
DESIGNER
Matthew Coe
DESIGN FIRM
PharmaDesign, Inc.
CLIENT/MFR
Somerset Pharmaceutical
AWARD
Bronze 1990

The Eldepryl Dispenser addresses the special needs of patients with Parkinson's disease for whom removing a small tablet from a prescription bottle is a difficult task. By holding the dispenser in one hand and pushing it across the palm of the other hand, the patient activates an internal wheel that turns, dispensing a single tablet.

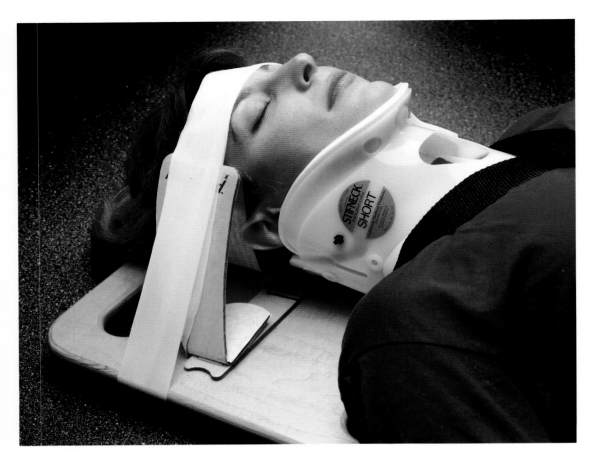

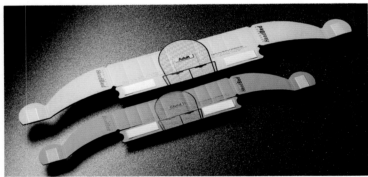

PRODUCT
Stifneck HeadBed™ CID
DESIGNER
Jim Traut
DESIGN FIRM
California Medical Products
CLIENT/MFR
California Medical Products
AWARD
Gold 1989

Designed to facilitate effective spinal immobilization, the Stifneck HeadBed addresses the critical problem of head immobilization and can be positioned under the head even after the patient is strapped to a standard spinal immobilization board. Made of die-cut corrugated board, the Stifneck HeadBed is disposable, stores compactly and is easy to use.

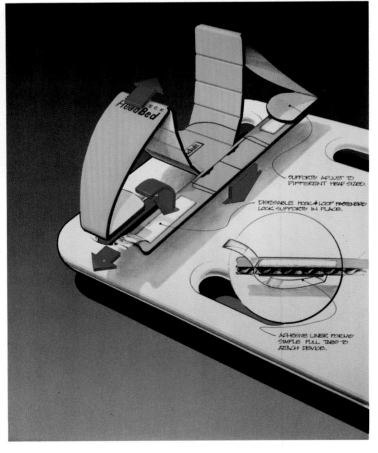

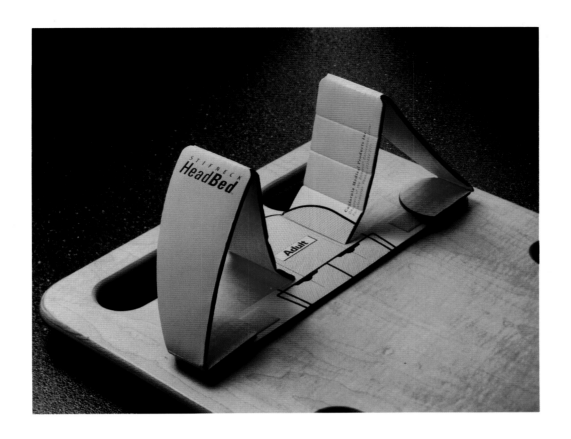

PRODUCT
1-Day and 14-Day Insulin Kits
DESIGNERS
James J. Costello, Ron Renkel,
J. A. Decker
DESIGN FIRM
Igloo Products Corporation
CLIENT/MFR
Igloo Products Corporation
AWARD
Silver 1989

This product organizes the diabetic's insulin, syringes and other implements in an anonymous, insulated, high-impact polystyrene case. Designed to hold either American or European vials, the Kit facilitates the use of insulin while traveling for up to 14 days.

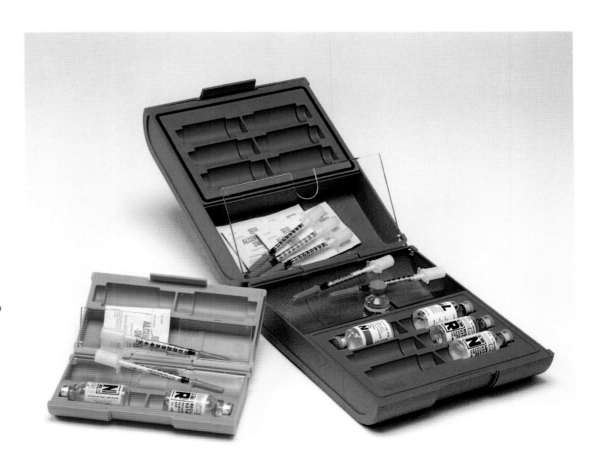

PRODUCT
VACUTAINER Brand Blood
Collection Tubes with Hemogard™
Closure
DESIGNERS
Chris Dufresne, Eric Frankel, Nick
Grippi
DESIGN FIRM
Becton Dickinson VACUTAINER
SYSTEMS
CLIENT/MFR
Becton Dickinson VACUTAINER
SYSTEMS
AWARD
Bronze 1990

The novel closure for VACU-
TAINER Brand Collection
Tubes provides a protective
barrier between the user and
the blood specimen. The rubber stopper that seals the
tube is covered by a plastic
shield.

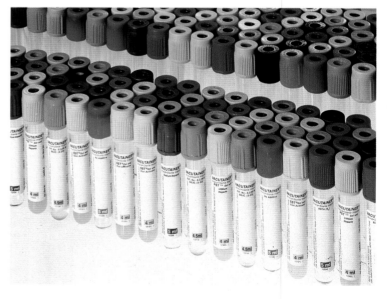

PRODUCT
Malaria Centrifuge and Microscope
DESIGNERS
Stephen G. Hauser, Manuel
Fernandez, Mark Schoening
DESIGN FIRM
S. G. Hauser Associates
CLIENT/MFR
Becton Dickinson and Company
AWARD
Bronze 1989

This easy-to-use, portable malaria test instrumentation kit is designed for detection of malaria in third world countries where early detection of the disease remains a continuing problem. The compact fluorescent microscope and centrifuge can be battery-operated and are contained in a rugged, waterproof carrying case.

PRODUCT
Hypothermia Suit for Stranded Motorists
DESIGNER
Rebecca Marie Stames while a student at Stanford University
AWARD
Silver 1989

Designed for any automobile operator or passenger driving in severe weather conditions, the Hypothermia Suit can be stored under the car seat until needed. Large openings with Velcro closures permit the user to enter the suit quickly and with confidence. Constructed of open-celled foam between two sheets of high strength material, the configuration of the suit allows the user to increase warmth by assuming the fetal position which reduces body heat loss by 50 percent.

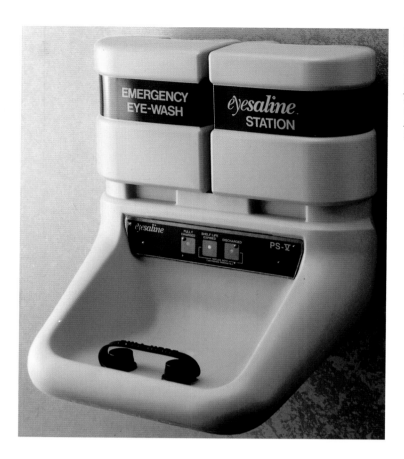

PRODUCT
Eyesaline Eyewash Station
DESIGNERS
Mike Joss, Stanley Gresens
DESIGN FIRM
Joss Design Group
CLIENT/MFR
Fendall Company
AWARD
Bronze 1989

The Eyesaline Eyewash Station provides a safety eyewash station for commercial and industrial work environments. Easy to operate, it features a wash solution that is safer to the eyes than water alone.

PRODUCT
Fire Extinguisher
DESIGNER
Donald Carr
AWARD
Bronze 1990

By simplifying operability, this fire extinguisher is designed to save valuable time and possibly a life in a panic situation. Moreover, the one-piece molded plastic part weighs less than a traditional metal cylinder, an important issue for both the young and elderly.

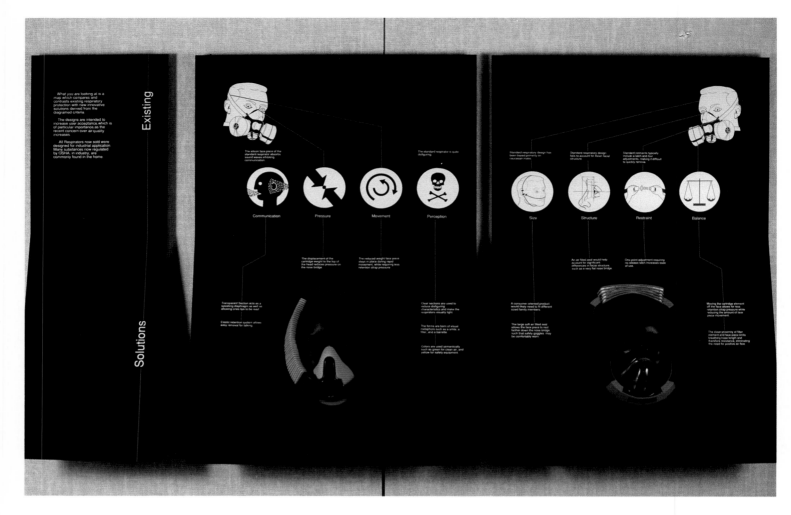

PRODUCT
Personal Respiratory Protection
DESIGNER
David Abkowitz while a graduate
student at Rochester Institute of
Technology
AWARD
Bronze 1989

This project examines ways
of increasing user accep-
tance of respiratory pro-
tection in an age when
chemicals pose increasing
health risks both at work and
in the home. The exhibit
compares and contrasts the
standard respirator with new
and innovative designs. A key
feature of the new designs is
the distribution of 50 percent
of the device weight off the
face, reducing pressure on
the nose bridge.

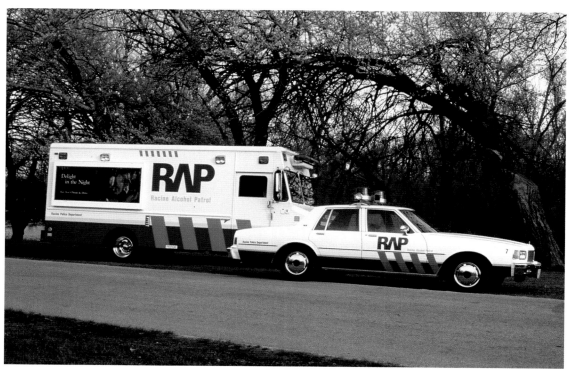

PRODUCT
Racine Alcohol Project (R.A.P.)
DESIGNER
Bruce L. Renquist
DESIGN FIRM
Renquist/Associates
CLIENT/MFR
Police Department, Racine, Wisconsin
AWARD
Bronze 1990

This program was developed to increase public awareness of the dangers of drinking and driving and to decrease the time required to process a DWI arrest. The project included coining the R.A.P. name, designing a vehicle for a mobile breath testing unit and designing a R.A.P. van to act as an educational tool and rolling billboard on the streets.

PRODUCT
Child Safety Rail System
DESIGNER
John J. Gatzemeyer while a student at Syracuse University
CLIENT/MFR
Juvenile Product Manufacturers Association
AWARD
Gold 1990

The Child Stair Rail fits onto an existing adult stair rail and promotes safety by helping a young child up or down a straight set of stairs. Modular in design and simple in construction, it can be sold in sectional sets to accommodate a variety of stair lengths and designs.

29

PRODUCT
Infant Car Seat
DESIGNER
Kenneth P. Morton
DESIGN FIRM
Fisher-Price
CLIENT/MFR
Fisher-Price
AWARD
Gold 1990

This Infant Car Seat combines automotive safety elements with infant and parental needs outside the car. The seat locks easily and securely to shopping carts by means of a spring-loaded ladder hook mechanism. Because it is convenient and inviting to use, it encourages car seat use.

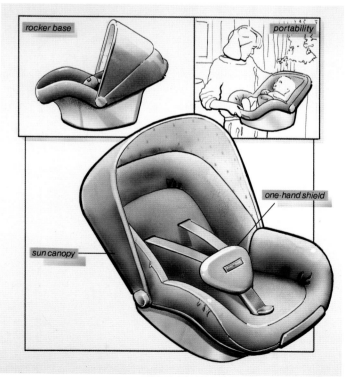

PRODUCT
Bag Hog
DESIGNERS
John Lonczak, Tony Baxter, Simon Yan
DESIGN FIRM
John Lonczak Design
CLIENT/MFR
Form Farm, Inc.
AWARD
Gold 1990

Bag Hog is a trash bag holder made of rugged recyclable polyethylene or recycled paperboard. It uses minimal materials, packaging and technology and requires less energy to make than a molded container. Its function as a recycle center and its own recyclability meets a timely need.

PRODUCT
Heller BagRecycler
DESIGNER
Morison S. Cousins
DESIGN FIRM
Cousins Design
CLIENT/MFR
Heller Designs
AWARD
Silver 1990

A storage and dispenser product, the Heller BagRecycler encourages reuse of plastic grocery bags. The simple container attaches inside a cabinet door or on the wall. Plastic bags are stuffed in at the top and then pulled, individually, from the bottom.

PRODUCT
5 Gallon Solution
DESIGNER
Paul Patrick Loduha while a student at the University of Illinois
AWARD
Silver 1990

The 5 Gallon Solution addresses the reuse of discarded five gallon buckets at construction sites. The design consists of nesting plastic inserts that can be used in various combinations to tailor the tool/hardware carrier to the needs of each user.

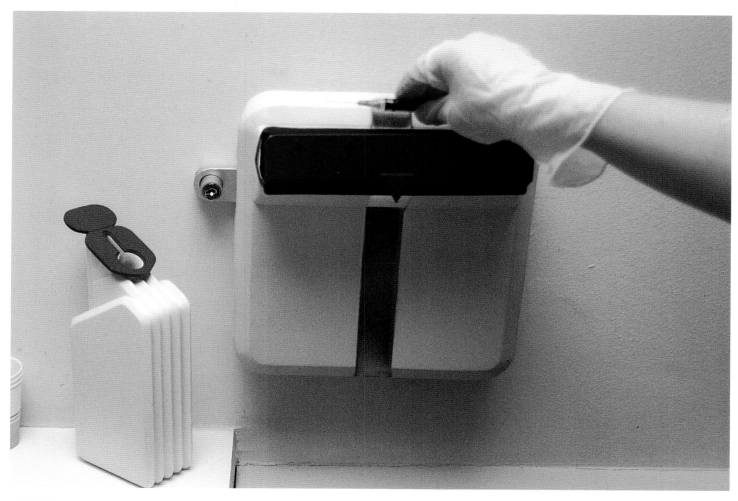

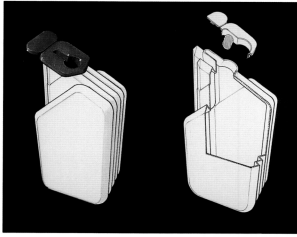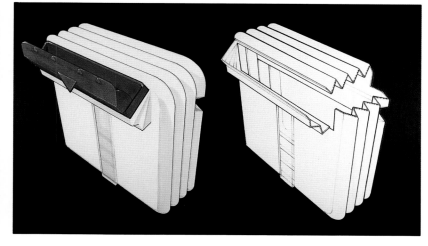

PRODUCT
Sharpsline Container System
DESIGNERS
Rita S. Graef and John E. Huetz while
students at the University of the Arts
CLIENT/MFR
Inter Metro Industries Corp.
AWARD
Bronze 1989

Sharpsline is a series of general and specific infectious waste containers for the disposal of needles, syringes and contaminated waste. The general use container is constructed to prevent needles from being over-stuffed and puncturing the bottom. The special use container is designed to meet the needs of the IV blood-drawing team: squeezable flutes serve as a wrench to remove the contaminated needle from its re-usable carrier.

PRODUCT
Tennison Toilet
DESIGNERS
Sam Disney, Andrew L. Alger
DESIGN FIRM
Goldsmith Yamasaki Specht, Inc.
CLIENT/MFR
Eljer Industries
AWARD
Bronze 1990

A vitreous china toilet with a one-piece low integral tank, the Tennison Toilet utilizes only 1.6 gallons of water to flush. Designed to operate quietly with a push button, the Tennison is also designed to achieve maximum productivity in casting and firing.

PRODUCT
Impact
DESIGNER
John R. Shinella
DESIGN FIRM
General Motors Design Staff
CLIENT/MFR
General Motors Corp.
AWARD
Bronze 1990

Probably the first electric vehicle to pay attention to aesthetics, this electric car achieves a 120 mile range between battery charges. Its aerodynamic efficiency is considerable, critical to achieve this range; it has a zero-degree-yaw drag coefficient of .19, half that of most production cars. The Impact repowers by being plugged into regular household current.

PRODUCT
Folding Bike
DESIGNER
Duenren Shiau while a student at the
Art Center College of Design
AWARD
Bronze 1989

Designed for the office worker's daily transportation between the parking lot or subway station and the office, the Folding Bike is lightweight, simple to fold and unfold, and easily carried. The construction utilizes graphite/epoxy composite over a honeycomb or foam core.

PRODUCT
4701 Activity Gym
DESIGNER
Kevin R. Aker
DESIGN FIRM
The Little Tikes Company Design Group
CLIENT/MFR
The Little Tikes Company
(a Rubbermaid Company)
AWARD
Silver 1988; IDSA Design of the Decade Award

The Little Tikes Activity Gym exemplifies responsible environmental design. It will last longer, without maintenance, than similar wood or steel gyms. It is inherently safer and its materials are benign as opposed to chemically-treated wood or potentially sharp and rusting steel. Moreover, the entire product can be recycled.

PRODUCT
Aqualine—R.O. Water Purifier
DESIGNER
Sohrab Vossoughi
DESIGN FIRM
Ziba Design
CLIENT/MFR
CD Medical, Inc.
AWARD
Silver 1989

The Aqualine—R.O. Water Purifier is an electronically monitored household water purifying system that utilizes the reverse osmosis filtering technology used in hemodialysis machines. The design uses rounded forms and pastel colors to enhance user friendliness.

PRODUCT
Clean Drinking Water System
DESIGNER
Jeffrey S. Rohrer
DESIGN FIRM
Regal Ware, Inc.
CLIENT/MFR
Club Watermasters, Inc.
AWARD
Bronze 1989

This system provides a simple way for today's homeowners to obtain clean, good-tasting drinking water. The unit offers consumers form, function and design, along with installation options, ease of operation and maintenance. The Clean Drinking Water System is a practical solution to an alarming environmental issue.

CHAPTER 2

CONSUMER PRODUCTS

FRESCO CRYSTAL GIFTWARE

"The simplicity of the forms in this glassware provides an elegance which enhances the marriage of product and environment."

—*Juror* **Patricia Moore,** IDSA

CLERET™ GLASS CLEANER

"It's a lyrical interpretation that shows design's ability to bring a joyous vision to unexpected places."

—*Juror* **V. Lorenzo Porcelli,** IDSA

PLYMOUTH LASER

"The Laser is a successful blend of performance and value with all the proper visual clues that should be present in this type of car."

—*Juror* **Clyde Foles,** IDSA

SPACEMAKER PLUS™

"This design's elegant restraint is exquisite."

—*Juror* **James Ryan,** IDSA

PRODUCT
Cleret™ Glass Cleaner
DESIGNERS
Sohrab Vossoughi, Christopher Alviar,
Paul Furner
DESIGN FIRM
Ziba Design
CLIENT/MFR
Hanco
AWARD
Gold 1989

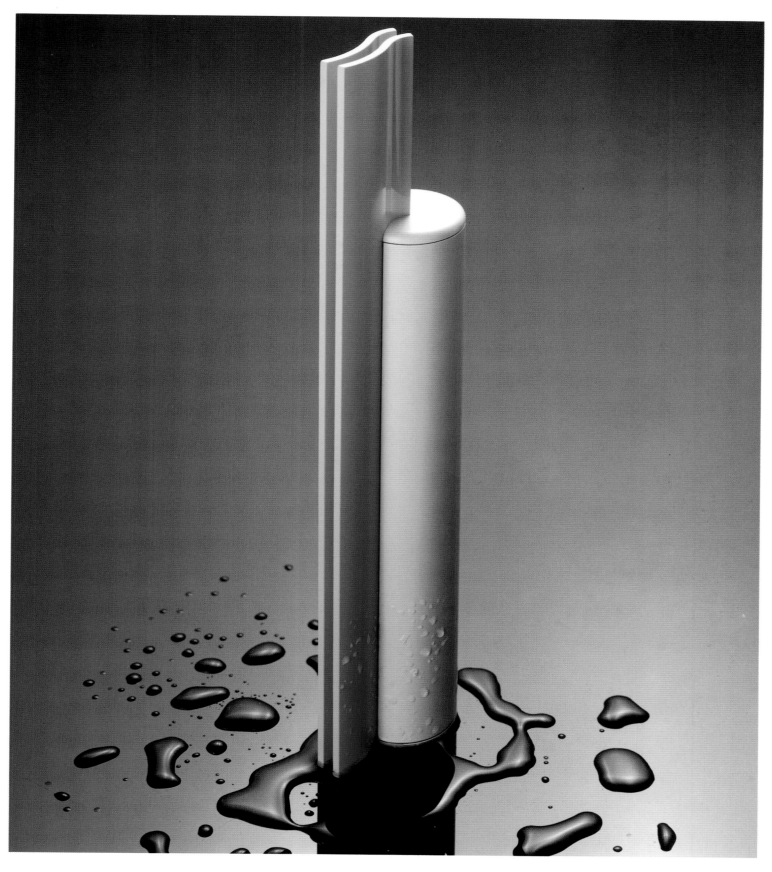

A household accessory for cleaning glass and mirrors, the Cleret Glass Cleaner was developed to fill the increasing need to dry custom glass shower enclosures. The cylindrical design is ergonomically sound, functionally simple and visually fresh.

PRODUCT
Geo Frame
DESIGNER
Nicolai Canetti
DESIGN FIRM
Canetti Group
CLIENT/MFR
Canetti, Inc.
AWARD
Bronze 1989

The almost frameless Geo Frame allows pictures to be displayed back to back in a horizontal or vertical format without any obstruction. Using glass and rubber, the design achieves a contemporary look while the weight of the rubber base provides stability.

PRODUCT
Fresco Crystal Giftware Collection
DESIGNER
Valerie L. Stone
DESIGN FIRM
Lenox China & Crystal
CLIENT/MFR
Lenox China & Crystal
AWARD
Gold 1990

The Fresco Crystal Giftware line is a collection of 24 percent lead crystal bowls, vases and a centerpiece comprising a decorative accessory line that is functional art. A slumped wall creates the "well" of the bowls and centerpiece; the form is inverted to create the vases.

PRODUCT
„Spacemaker Plus™
DESIGNERS
Don R. McCloskey, Sally A. Hattle,
Gary Van Deursen; Group 4 and
John Howard Design
DESIGN FIRMS
Black & Decker US Household
Group; Group 4; John Howard
Design
CLIENT/MFR
Black & Decker US Household Group
AWARD
Gold 1988

An integrated system of
under-the-cabinet kitchen
products, Spacemaker Plus
includes a coffeemaker, can
opener/knife sharpener and
task light. The design creates
and conveys efficient use of
space in the work environment. Moreover, the design
makes it easy to safely insert
and withdraw the carafe.

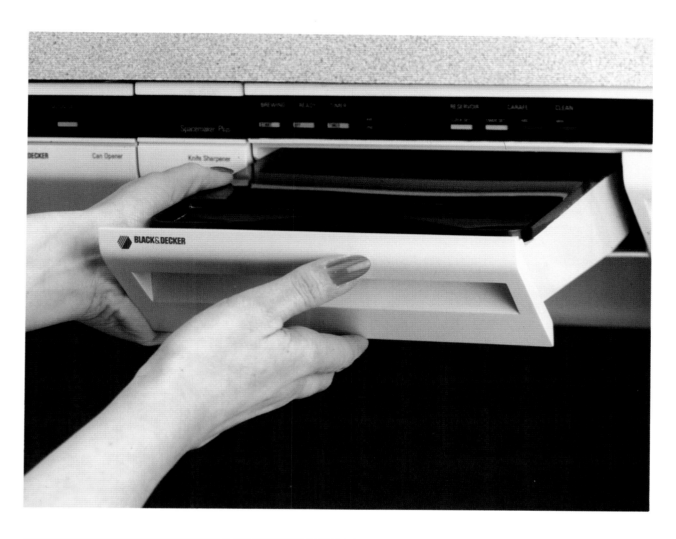

PRODUCT
Sid Containers
DESIGNER
Sid Shakir
DESIGN FIRM
Sid Containers
CLIENT/MFR
Midwest Plastics, Inc.
AWARD
Bronze 1990

This clear polycarbonate tray holds silverware off the tablecloth while eating, thereby helping maintain a tidy table area. It is especially useful for weaker individuals and children.

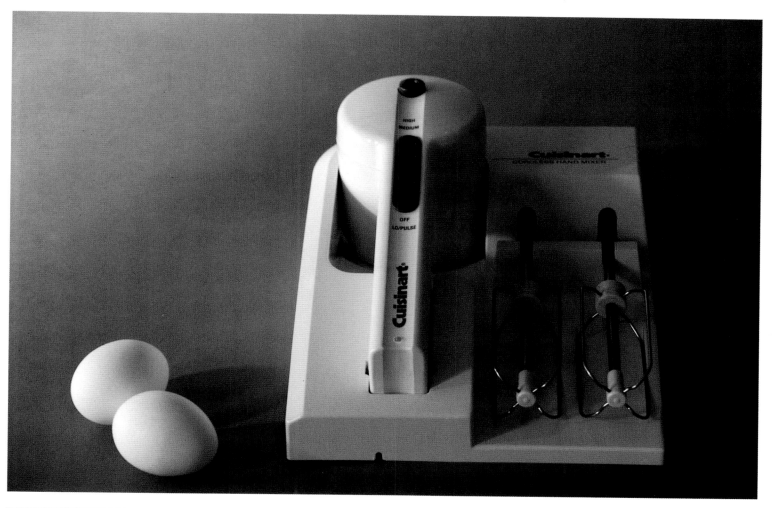

PRODUCT
Hand Mixer
DESIGNERS
Paul Corsi, Michael Hissong,
Steve Leonard
DESIGN FIRM
ID Product Development, Inc. (IDC)
CLIENT/MFR
Cuisinarts, Inc.
AWARD
Bronze 1989

This hand mixer features high-performance components in a housing designed to accentuate control and minimize user stress. Cordless, with a comfortable handle, it can be used continuously on a high or medium setting or in a pulse mode at low speed.

PRODUCT
Counter Top Can Opener
DESIGNERS
Randall Bell, Ralph LaZar
DESIGN FIRM
Herbst LaZar Bell, Inc.
CLIENT/MFR
Waring Products Division, Dynamics Corporation of America
AWARD
Silver 1988

A clean, contemporary can opener based on an existing mechanism, the Counter Top Can Opener is capable of opening taller cans without appearing massive or cumbersome.

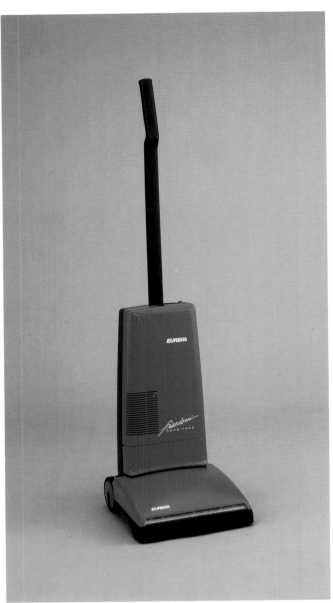

PRODUCT
Freedom Cord Free Upright Vacuum
Cleaner
DESIGNERS
Kenneth R. Parker, Sue Pike
DESIGN FIRM
The Eureka Company
CLIENT/MFR
The Eureka Company
AWARD
Silver 1990

The Freedom is the world's
first battery-powered,
full-sized upright vacuum
cleaner. Easy to use, simple
to recharge and convenient
to store, it has the cleaning
capabilities of a corded vacuum and a sufficient run
time to clean an average
house on a single charge.

PRODUCT
Folding Ironing Board
DESIGNERS
David Dombrowski, David Reid and
Keith Christopher while students at
the University of Bridgeport
CLIENT/MFR
Black & Decker, Inc.
AWARD
Bronze 1990

This design represents a new
and innovative way to use,
fold and store an ironing
board. The board rolls, opens
and closes easily and has an
effective height adjustment
feature. Because it doesn't
need to be lifted and it can
be rolled with minimal effort,
it has appeal for the elderly
and the disabled.

PRODUCT
Home Pro Garden Tool Line
DESIGNERS
James E. Grove, John Cook,
Jim Holtorf, Fernando Pardo,
Mike Botich
DESIGN FIRM
DESIGNWORKS/USA
CLIENT/MFR
Corona Clipper Company
AWARD
Silver 1990

This design demonstrates a
true concern for ergonomics.
In developing the Corona
Home Pro Garden Tool Line,
the design team evaluated
over 150 existing garden
tools. Subtleties in the handle shapes reflect this
thorough investigation.
Santoprene was utilized in
the grip areas to provide a
soft, tactile, non-slip surface,
helping to reduce blisters
and hand fatigue.

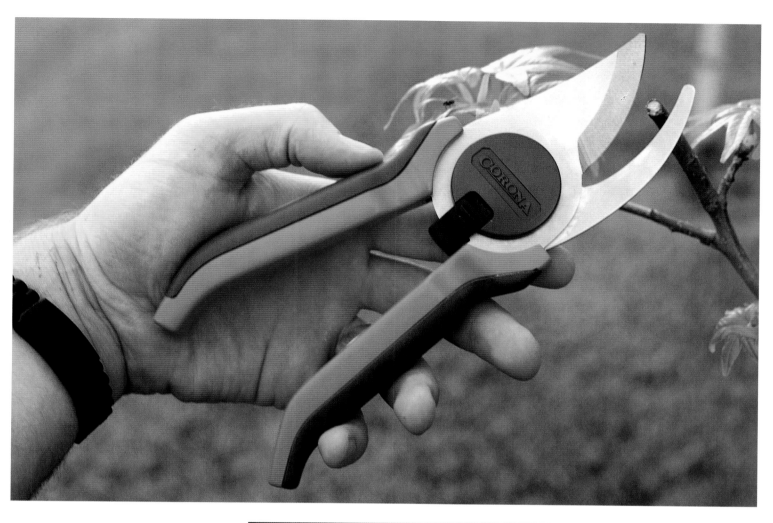

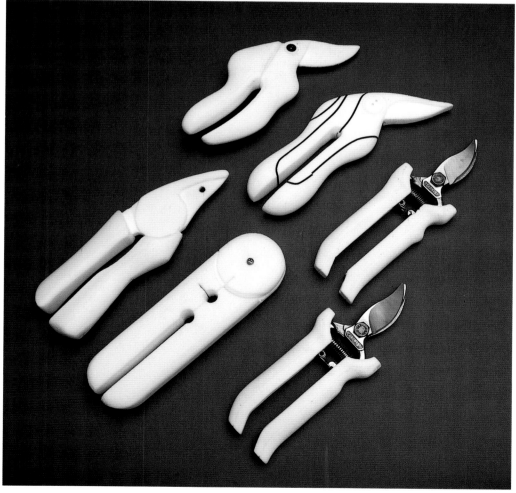

PRODUCT
John Deere Front Mower
DESIGNERS
William Crookes, Lawrence Sliker,
Kevin Thompson
DESIGN FIRM
Henry Dreyfuss Associates
CLIENT/MFR
Deere & Company
AWARD
Bronze 1989

A maneuverable and efficient mowing machine, the John Deere Front Mower is a residential-class riding mower that provides the performance of a commercial product. Relocating the mower deck in front improves maneuverability and provides better visibility for the operator.

PRODUCT
Scotts Cartridge Spreader
DESIGNERS
Donald J. Rebele, David B. Chaney
DESIGN FIRM
The Corporate Design Center, Inc.
CLIENT/MFR
O. M. Scott and Sons
AWARD
Silver 1988

The Scotts Cartridge Spreader is used to safely and efficiently broadcast bottled dry fertilizer on up to 5,000 square feet of lawn and is designed specifically for the consumer who is concerned about safely using and storing chemical fertilizers. Because the fertilizer cartridge plugs directly into the spreader, no handling of the chemical is necessary.

PRODUCT
Essentials Home Maintenance Kit
DESIGNERS
Stanley Tools New Product
Development Group, and Group
Four Design
DESIGN FIRMS
Stanley Tools; Group Four Design
CLIENT/MFR
Stanley Tools, Division of the
Stanley Works
AWARD
Silver 1988

Designed to satisfy the
needs of the light do-it-your-
selfer, the Essentials Home
Maintenance Kit is a collection of tools, accessories and
information organized in a
portable carrying case. Mul-
tiple materials and processes
were used to create these
functional yet aesthetically
appealing tools.

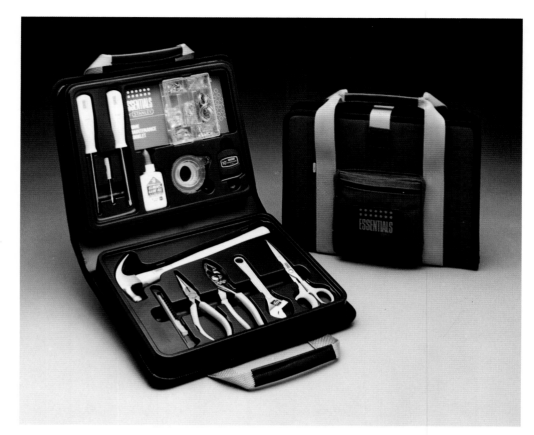

PRODUCT
Powercurve 1800 Electric
Snowthrower
DESIGNER
Tony Pink
DESIGN FIRM
The Toro Company
CLIENT/MFR
The Toro Company, Home
Improvement Division
AWARD
1989 Bronze

A lightweight electric snowthrower, the Powercurve addresses a new spectrum of
intended users—women, the
elderly and owners of small
lots. The design conveys
both user friendliness and
the machine's aggressive
ability to perform its task.

PRODUCT
Becker EC Phone
DESIGNER
Eric P. Chan
DESIGN FIRM
Chan + Dolan Design
CLIENT/MFR
Becker, Inc.
AWARD
Silver 1989

The profile of the Becker EC Phone is the result of thorough human factors research. It provides the perfect angle for hearing and speaking, and the handset features a soft rubber face for ear comfort.

PRODUCT
Series I 10 × 42 Binoculars
DESIGNER
Steven Shull
DESIGN FIRM
Hanimex-Vivitar Group
CLIENT/MFR
Vivitar Corporation
AWARD
Silver 1989

These simple yet sophisticated binoculars for nature viewing, sports and amateur astronomy feature strong design details including electroformed coined nameplate, a diagonal rib detail and clean, fine-textured surfaces.

PRODUCT
X-300 Compact Camera
DESIGNERS
James E. Grove, Fernando Pardo, Steven Shull
DESIGN FIRMS
DESIGNWORKS/USA and Hanimex-Vivitar Group
CLIENT/MFR
Vivitar Corporation
AWARD
Bronze 1989

An automatic focus snapshot camera intended for family use, the X-300 is an attractive, affordable camera with a unique, simple design and good ergonomics.

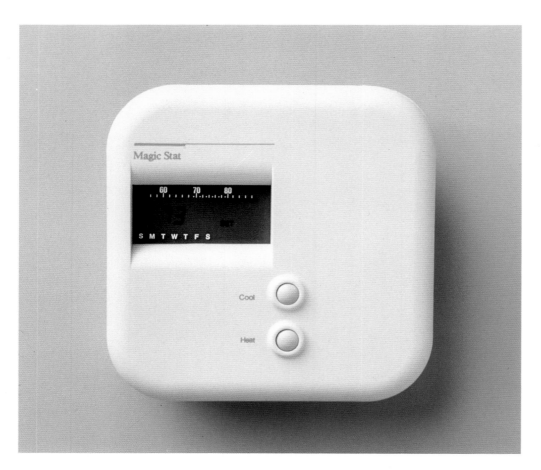

PRODUCT
Thermostat (3100)
DESIGNERS
Michael A. Cousins, June Lee
DESIGN FIRM
Cousins Design
CLIENT/MFR
Honeywell
AWARD
Bronze 1989

Representing state-of-the-art technology, this home thermostat is designed to fit all locations, whether traditional or contemporary. It is programmable for seven-day cycles, allowing manual override without affecting long-term programming.

PRODUCT
VR 480 VCR
DESIGNERS
Thomas Edward Renk, Jr.,
Richard Bourgerie
DESIGN FIRM
Thomson Consumer Electronics
CLIENT/MFR
Thomson Consumer Electronics
AWARD
Bronze 1989

The VR 480 VCR is designed to offer ease of use, avoiding the visual intimidation and proliferation of controls normally associated with audio/video equipment. To simplify the appearance, only the primary controls are exposed, with secondary controls grouped under the secondary control door.

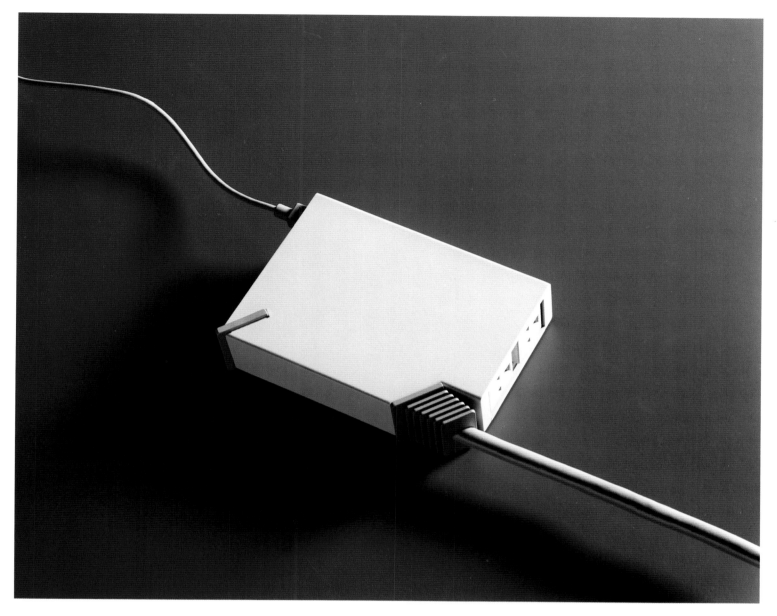

PRODUCT
Power Key
DESIGNERS
Nick Barker, Loyd Moore, Jeff Brown
DESIGN FIRM
Technology Design
CLIENT/MFR
Sophisticated Circuits
AWARD
Bronze 1990

This product enables the Macintosh Computer to be turned on directly from the keyboard instead of reaching around to the back of the computer. It is also a high-quality surge suppressor. The colored cable provides an easily identifiable method of sorting out the cables behind the computer.

PRODUCT
Expander Programmable Sprinkler
Controller
DESIGNERS
Robert Brunner, Ken Wood
DESIGN FIRM
Lunar Design
CLIENT/MFR
The Toro Company
AWARD
Silver 1989

A control device for residential sprinkler systems, the Toro Expander Programmable Sprinkler Controller is a departure from the "generic green boxes" that most people have adopted for sprinkler controllers. It is sophisticated in appearance and easy to use; only three basic ideas need to be remembered in order to operate the program.

PRODUCT
Plymouth Laser/Mitsubishi Eclipse
DESIGNERS
Chrysler Design Staff/Mitsubishi
Cypress, CA, Design Staff
CLIENT/MFR
Diamond Star Motors
AWARD
Gold 1989

An affordable sporty car, the Laser/Eclipse presents a fresh design with "fun to drive" appeal. It combines modern, sleek aerodynamic forms with high-tech performance. Wheels and tires are pulled out flush to the body in keeping with the flush, smooth handling of details used throughout the car's design.

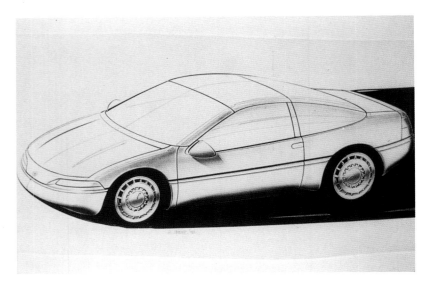

PRODUCT
1988 Pontiac Grand Prix
DESIGN FIRM
General Motors Design Staff
CLIENT/MFR
Pontiac Motor Division
AWARD
Silver 1988

The Pontiac Grand Prix is a sporty, mid-sized coupe designed to look aggressive and engineered to offer outstanding performance. A prominent grille and "below-the-bumper snout" give this car an instantly recognizable face. Its excellent aerodynamics were achieved through an unprecedented amount of wind-tunnel testing.

PRODUCT
1989 Ford Thunderbird
DESIGNERS
J.J. Telnack, F. C. Mayhew,
G. L. Halderman
DESIGN FIRM
Ford Motor Company Design Center
CLIENT/MFR
Ford Motor Company
AWARD
Bronze 1989

This distinctive, trend-setting four-wheel-drive vehicle is intended to appeal to up-scale, sophisticated consumers desiring a car that is functionally superior and exciting to drive. The overall design improves aerodynamics, reduces wind noise and improves fuel economy. Moreover, the low cowl and belt line placement improve driver sight lines and safety.

PRODUCT
CQ10 Graphic Equalizer, CA212
Power Amp., CR151 In-Dash Cassette
DESIGNERS
Daniel Ashcraft, Dan Wickemeyer
DESIGN FIRM
Ashcraft Design
CLIENT/MFR
Harman Kardon
AWARD
Silver 1988

Traditional in-dash units have an area of individual small buttons and features. The CR151 integrates the form into the buttons giving the user larger, easier-to-access functions. This also visually simplifies already cluttered dashboards.

PRODUCT
1988 Oldsmobile Cutlass Supreme
DESIGN FIRM
General Motors Design Staff
CLIENT/MFR
Oldsmobile Motor Division
AWARD
1988 Gold

An elegant and distinctive mid-sized car, the Cutlass Supreme was designed to appeal to the mature, traditional Oldsmobile customer as well as to a new audience. The exterior is restrained and elegant; the interior is tailored, offering six-way power seats with lumbar support, headrest positioning and side bolster adjustment.

PRODUCT
Comp T/A HR
DESIGNER
Dennis W. Krupa
DESIGN FIRM
BF Goodrich, now Uniroyal Goodrich
CLIENT/MFR
BF Goodrich, now Uniroyal Goodrich
AWARD
Silver 1988

A tire for high-performance automobiles, the Comp T/R HR features excellent handling, durability, snow traction, wet traction and high-speed handling. Its innovative, aggressive, organically shaped block design, integrated with a five rib curvilinear design, produces exceptional results.

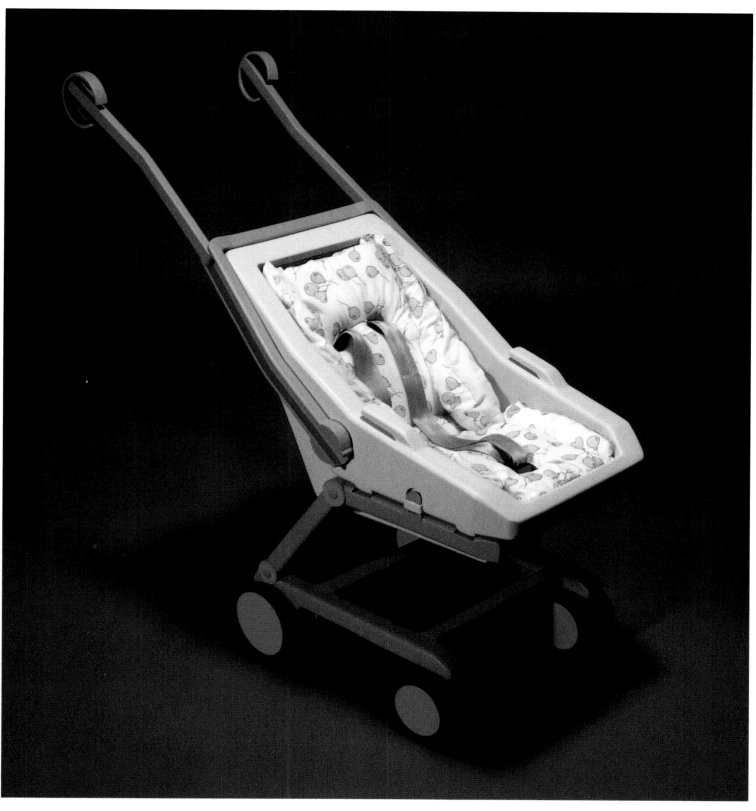

PRODUCT
KAR-CEET
DESIGNER
Clay Johnson while a student at
Auburn University
AWARD
Bronze 1989

Combining an auto safety
seat, stroller and infant
carrier all in one unit,
KAR-CEET eliminates the
need to transfer the infant
from the auto safety seat to
a separate stroller. It also reduces the number of accessories that parents and
caregivers need to transport
when traveling with an
infant.

C H A P T E R 3

SPORTS AND RECREATION

SPORTSCOPE

"*This product exhibits a playful, sophisticated solution to a playful, sophisticated toy.*"

—*Juror* **Brian Kane,** IDSA

AQUA COLOR BOX

"*Here is a design solution that is elegant, cost-effective and functional.*"

—*Juror* **David Tompkins,** FIDSA

VOYAGER

"*The Voyager's stimulating visual impact and innovative combination of form and color enhance the functions of touching, listening and speaking.*"

—*Juror* **Jack Kelley,** IDSA

PRODUCT
Kryptolite 6000 Hockey Stick
DESIGNERS
Robert J. De brey, Kirk Schneider
DESIGN FIRM
De brey Design
CLIENT/MFR
Northland Sports, Inc.
AWARD
Bronze 1989

Used by high school, college and pro players, the "Kryptolite" hockey stick represents a dramatic improvement in strength and durability. These qualities are made possible by "SPECTRA" filament, a new high-strength wonder fiber. The vibrant fluorescent green "super logo" was designed to increase brand name readability during ice play.

PRODUCT
Protech II Hardsided Golfbag
DESIGNERS
Young S. Kim, Bill Jones
DESIGN FIRM
INNO Design, Inc.
CLIENT/MFR
INNO Design, Inc.
AWARD
Bronze 1990

A revolutionary all-plastic golf bag, the Protech II affords golf travelers maximum protection with minimum weight. The two molded hardcover halves, attached to the main bag with a double hinge assembly, can be removed for lighter and easier use of the golf bag on the golf course.

PRODUCT
Hillcrest Motorcaddie
DESIGNERS
Edgar Montague, Eddie Machen,
James Machen
DESIGN FIRM
Machen Montague
CLIENT/MFR
Kangaroo Products
AWARD
Bronze 1989

The Hillcrest Motorcaddie carries a bag of golf clubs and is powered for use on the steepest hills. The designers arranged the power and steering controls so that, unlike its predecessor, it can be operated with one hand. It is easily disassembled into three lightweight parts; two motorcaddies and golf bags are readily accommodated in a compact car trunk.

PRODUCT
Husski Ski Valet
DESIGNERS
Peter W. Bressler,
Peter D. Byar
DESIGN FIRM
Bresslergroup
CLIENT/MFR
Magwin Enterprises
AWARD
Silver 1988

The Husski Ski Valet assists in transporting skis, boots, poles and ski accessories. Lightweight and easy to use, it can be car topped and also fits airline baggage requirements. The assemblage is pulled and steered by the ski tips and can negotiate over gravel, mud, deep snow and up and down steps.

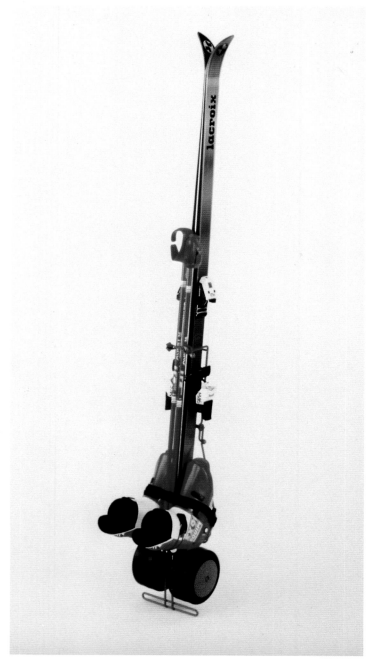

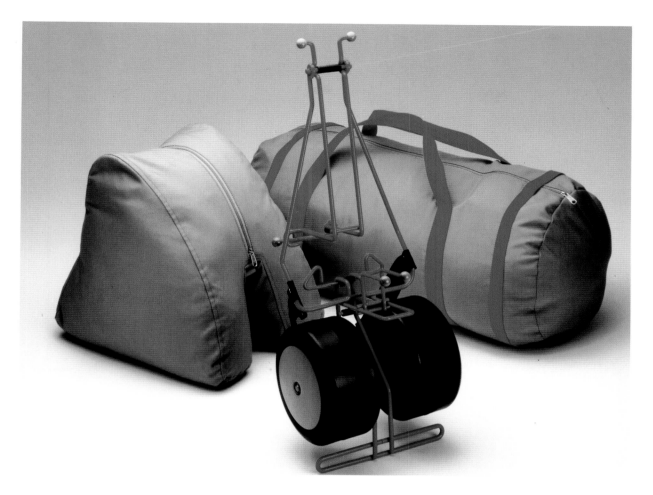

PRODUCT
Olympic Two-Man Bobsled
DESIGNERS
Sheryl A. Mulne-Derrow,
Joel M. Smith and Barry Smith while
students at Ohio State University.
CLIENT/MFR
Ron and Bob Horvath—
Youngstown, Ohio
AWARD
Silver 1988

The design for this bobsled achieved a 25-percent reduction in the coefficient of drag (in one-third scale) during wind tunnel testing. The form, unlike other cowlings, resembles a teardrop rather than a bullet configuration. The nose is relatively full and the sled is rounded all over as opposed to straight sided.

PRODUCT
Fitness Monitor Model 500
DESIGNERS
Sohrab Vossoughi, Henry Chin,
Christopher Alviar
DESIGN FIRM
Ziba Design
CLIENT/MFR
NIKE, Inc.
AWARD
Bronze, 1989

A waist-worn electronic measuring device for exercise and fitness, the NIKE Monitor 500 provides users with information on distance traveled, time, speed, and heart rate. Pressing a button accesses information through a high-resolution LCD display. To minimize any hesitation a user might have in "wearing a machine," a simple organic shape was designed to humanize the complex technology it houses.

PRODUCT
Tailwind
DESIGNER
Sohrab Vossoughi, Paul Furner
DESIGN FIRM
Ziba Design
CLIENT/MFR
Pro-Form Industries
AWARD
Silver 1988

Tailwind is an easy-to-use and highly adjustable stationary exercise cycle designed to meet the needs of both male and female athletes. The "step-through" frame design makes Tailwind less intimidating for users who are less fit.

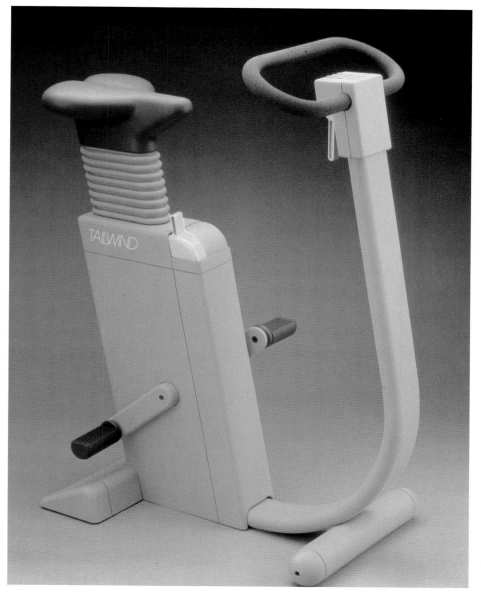

PRODUCT
The Step
DESIGNERS
William J. Saunders, Samuel C. Crosby
DESIGN FIRM
Industrial Design Assoc., Inc.
CLIENT/MFR
Sports Step, Inc.
AWARD
Bronze 1990

The Step Exercise System provides a total fitness workout which involves stepping on and off a height-adjustable platform. The design translated the plywood crates used in local health clubs into a form suitable to serve a larger market.

PRODUCT
Kestrel MX-Z Mountain Bicycle
DESIGNER
H.G. Wells
DESIGN FIRM
Kennedy Design
CLIENT/MFR
Cycle Composites, Inc. (Division of Schwinn)
AWARD
Bronze 1989

A strong, lightweight plastic bicycle for pleasure and competition, the Kestrel features a single-piece, molded-graphite-fiber mountain bike frame presenting a smooth, aerodynamic appearance.

PRODUCT
Dodge Viper R/T Show Vehicle
DESIGN FIRM
Chrysler Design Staff
CLIENT/MFR
Chrysler Motors
AWARD
Silver 1989

This vehicle captures the true essence of a sports car, a simple and direct interface between driver and vehicle, with a minimum of frills and high-tech hardware.

PRODUCT
Pontiac Stinger
DESIGN FIRM
General Motors Design Staff
CLIENT/MFR
Pontiac Motor Division
AWARD
Silver 1989

The innovative Stinger has been described as a "Swiss army knife on wheels." Its body is comprised of carbon-fiber panels and removable glass panels in different combinations. This transforms the Stinger from an enclosed, two-door car to an open-air sport or utility vehicle. Included in its multiplicity of features are: a cellular phone, message machine, compass, seats that transform into lawn chairs, fire extinguishers, and picnic kits.

PRODUCT
g.Analyst
DESIGNERS
Thomas David, Peter Koloski,
Bob Hayes, Jeff Pacione
DESIGN FIRM
RichardsonSmith, Inc.
CLIENT/MFR
Valentine Research, Inc.
AWARD
Silver 1988

The g.Analyst is a device for
amateur racers and driving
enthusiasts that measures,
records and displays, numer-
ically and graphically, the
forces the driver and car experience during acceleration,
braking and turning. Operation of the device is similar
to a VCR or tape recorder.

PRODUCT
19CSS (Carlson Signature Series)
DESIGNER
Art Carlson
DESIGN FIRM
International Marine Designs, Inc.
CLIENT/MFR
Glastron, Inc.
AWARD
Bronze 1989

This boat is both aero-
dynamically and hydro-
dynamically designed. One
of its major features is the
ski arch which incorporates
the optimal point of towing
water skiers with an aerodynamic wing section. The boat
includes an enclosed forward
berth not usually found on
vessels in this size class.

PRODUCT
O'Day 322
DESIGNERS
Charles W. Kellstedt, Jr., Joel Lieblein
DESIGN FIRM
Gunn Associates
CLIENT/MFR
The O'Day Corporation
AWARD
Silver 1988

This cruising sailboat has a contemporary European look. The use of three values of gray on the exterior combined with tinted full-length, wrap-over side glass gives the boat a non-traditional appearance that distinguishes it from its competitors.

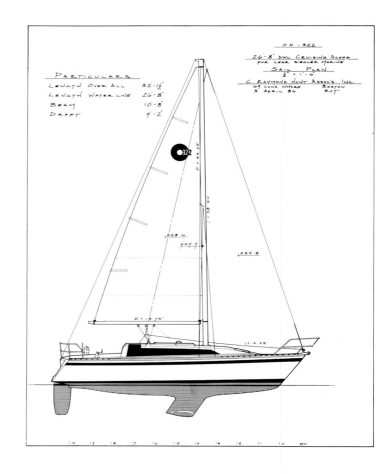

PRODUCT
12 Meter Express, Model 400
DESIGNERS
David C. Trost, Robert Peffer,
Robert Ray
DESIGN FIRM
Trojan Yacht Division of
Bertram-Trojan, Inc.
CLIENT/MFR
Trojan Yacht Division of
Bertram-Trojan, Inc.
AWARD
Silver 1989

European styling characterizes the interior and exterior detailing of this sophisticated pleasure boat and marine home. The design promotes ease of operation, safety and convenient maintenance. Helm visibility is improved through a new, electrically operated seat mechanism, and boarding is improved through concealed cockpit boarding steps and safety rails.

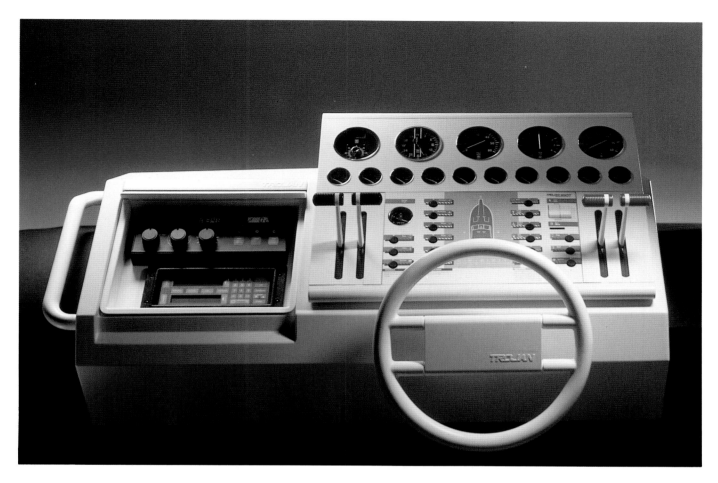

PRODUCT
Control Consoles
DESIGNERS
Spencer Murrell, Ken Brazell,
Jaimie Alexander
DESIGN FIRM
Fitch RichardsonSmith Inc.
CLIENT/MFR
Trojan Yacht Division of Bertram-
Trojan, Inc.
AWARD
Silver 1989

This design approach for the controls area of a line of motor yachts features a system of three modular parts: a fiberglass console, a control pod, and an equipment locker. The fiberglass console is the changeable part of the system that enables the control pod/locker(s) combination to fit a variety of decks.

PRODUCT
Chartviewer
DESIGNERS
Loyd Moore, Jeff Brown, Mark Eike
DESIGN FIRM
Technology Design
CLIENT/MFR
In Focus Systems
AWARD
Bronze 1989

Chartviewer is a fully portable, weatherproof, navigational map for the 30 foot and above boating market. It displays National Oceanic and Atmospheric Administration-based charts on a backlit LCD screen enabling the boater to locate position, plot a course and store it on the integral 3-1/2" disk drive.

PRODUCT
Autopilot Control Design System
DESIGNER
Vladymir Rogov
DESIGN FIRM
Rogov
CLIENT/MFR
Benmar
AWARD
Silver 1989

This modular, self-contained Autopilot steers a power boat, freeing the captain to mingle with friends. It can be mounted as a stand-alone assembly, or it can be flush mounted on a wall or control area at the helm. By pressing the appropriate controls, the captain programs the Autopilot and is free to roam with or without the remote handset.

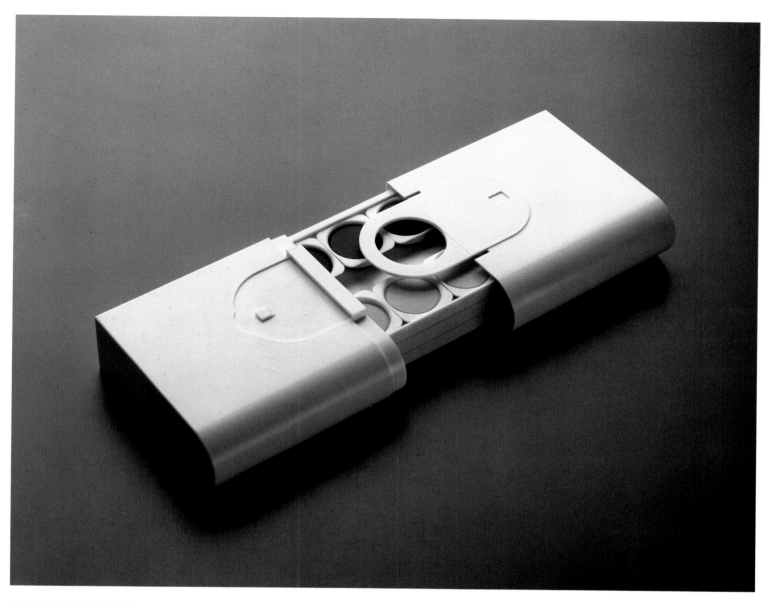

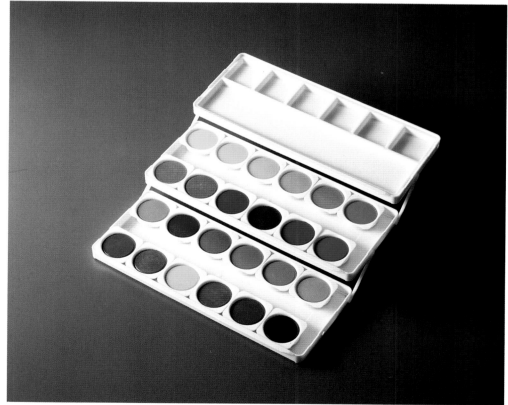

PRODUCT
Herlitz Aqua Color Box
DESIGNER
Emilio Ambasz
DESIGN FIRM
Emilio Ambasz Design Group
CLIENT/MFR
Herlitz GmbH
AWARD
Gold 1988

The Herlitz Aqua Color Box
provides a complete water
painting system. The three-
tiered, hinged palette and
color trays feature color pans
and a palette insert that may
be removed for cleaning or
replacement. The box itself is
a separate item whose two
halves join together to form
two vessels, one for water,
one to store brushes.

PRODUCT
My Frame
DESIGNERS
Tom Dair, Stephan Allendorf,
Tucker Viemeister
DESIGN FIRM
Smart Design, Inc.
CLIENT/MFR
My Art
AWARD
Bronze 1989

My Frame is a unique framing system that allows children to frame their own artwork. Easy to use, it is assembled by placing flat artwork on the white backing tray and then placing the clear cover sheet on top. The sandwich is held together by snapping on brightly colored moldings. In addition to providing fun, My Frame enhances children's independence and self-esteem.

PRODUCT
Voyager
DESIGNERS
James Couch, Elizabeth B.-N. Sanders,
Keith Kresge
DESIGN FIRM
RichardsonSmith, Inc.
CLIENT/MFR
Texas Instruments
AWARD
Gold 1988

A speech-interactive educational toy, Voyager combines form, texture and color in an innovative, safe product that appeals to children and parents. It is designed to accommodate a wide range of capabilities and limitations of the intended user and is adaptive in terms of fit, comfort and the cognitive challenges it offers.

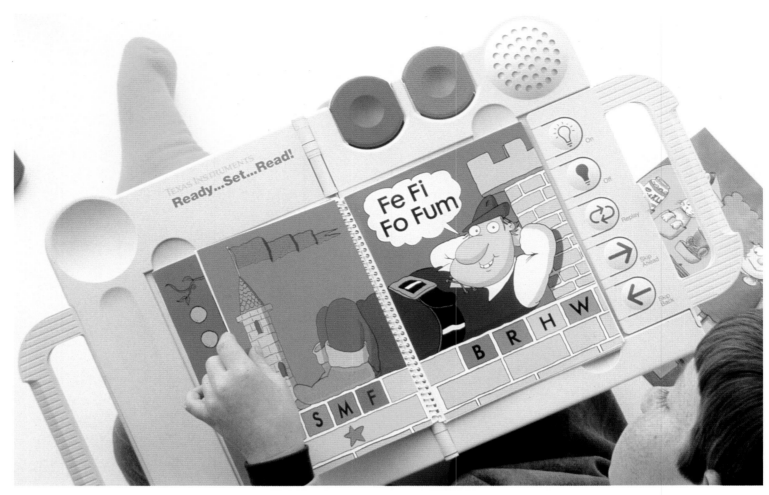

PRODUCT
READY...SET...READ!
DESIGN FIRM
Texas Instruments Corporate Design
Center
CLIENT/MFR
Texas Instruments
AWARD
Silver 1988

This educational product
helps children three to seven
develop important skills in
letter recognition, vocabulary, and reading. Its whimsi-
cal, animated appearance
suggests a fun-to-play-with
and fun-to-learn-from product that doesn't intimidate
children through its
technology.

PRODUCT
Super Speak & Spell
DESIGNERS
Khodi Feiz, Bill Dolan
DESIGN FIRM
Texas Instruments Corporate Design
Center
CLIENT/MFR
Texas Instruments
AWARD
Bronze 1989

An educational product for
children six through twelve,
Super Speak & Spell helps
children practice spelling
and build vocabulary. The
keyboard is simple and
highly understandable, with
highlighting on vowel keys,
making it easier for children
to locate the more frequently
used letters.

PRODUCT
TO GO!
DESIGNER
Kazu Amemiya, Khodi Feiz, Bill Dolan
DESIGN FIRM
Texas Instruments Corporate Design Center
CLIENT/MFR
Texas Instruments

An educational electronic toy, To Go! addresses spelling, time telling and math. Colorful images on coded cards are selected and placed over the Mylar keyboard; pressing the images activates an LC Display. Case colors play an important role in product differentiation and add a fun look.

PRODUCT
Screamers Stunt Kites
DESIGNER
Robert J. Mileti
DESIGN FIRM
Trlby Products Incorporated
CLIENT/MFR
The Great American Kite Company
AWARD
Bronze 1989

The Screamers Stunt Kites are Dual Line Controllable Kites developed for the mass market. They feature combined sail/instruction sheets, a patented bridle/link system, and a patented frame system. They require no critical assembly or adjustments to fly, perform well, are durable and can withstand repeated crashes.

PRODUCT
Sport Coupe
DESIGNERS
Kevin R. Aker, Robert L. Quinlan
DESIGN FIRM
The Little Tikes Company Design Group
CLIENT/MFR
The Little Tikes Company (a Rubbermaid Company)
AWARD
Silver 1988

This Sport Coupe is a simple, safe and fun pedal-drive vehicle for children aged three to six. The wide tires, wide track design, and low center of gravity of the rider's position render the Sport Coupe exceptionally stable.

PRODUCT
Sportscope
DESIGNERS
Robert Brunner, Ken Wood
DESIGN FIRM
Lunar Design
CLIENT/MFR
Carolina Pacific
AWARD
Gold 1989

The Sportscope is a high-quality, plastic periscope for use by individuals ages six and up. It is adjustable to allow viewing over different sizes of obstacles and to facilitate packing for travel.

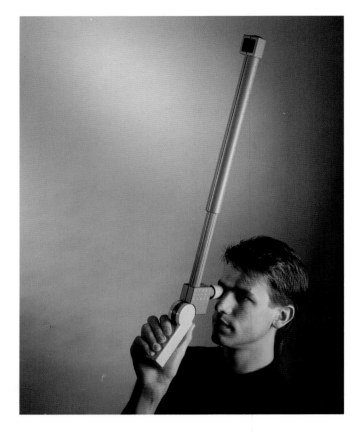

C H A P T E R **4**

COMPUTERS AND OFFICE EQUIPMENT

SIGMA NON-IMPACT PRINTER

"The Sigma is a beautiful product that maintains its own distinct identity, while elegantly complementing its environment. The designers' concern for detail and harmony combine to achieve excellence."

—*Juror* **Jack Beduhn**, IDSA

VUE 2.0 VISUAL USER ENVIRONMENT

"Part of the excellence of this design solution is that it appears deceptively simple, offering a representation of the functionality that is easy to grasp and quick to learn. Like many creative leaps forward, it seems obvious now that we can see it."

—*Juror* **Bill Moggridge**, IDSA

PRODUCT
MON 1649 Full-Page Monitor
DESIGNER
Lawrence M. Kuba
DESIGN FIRM
Wang Laboratories, Inc.
CLIENT/MFR
Wang Laboratories, Inc.
AWARD
Silver 1988

The MON 1640 is a 16-inch, black-and-white CRT display used in conjunction with the Wang Integrated Image Systems as a primary means of displaying high-resolution images. It will display a full page of text or images as well as having windowing capabilities. Recessed connectors in the back are easily accessed and allow the monitor to be pushed up against the wall without interference from cables.

PRODUCT
Emily & Julie Computer Keyboard & Monitor
DESIGNER
Loyd Moore
DESIGN FIRM
Technology Design
CLIENT/MFR
Synapse Products
AWARD
Bronze 1989

The design for this computer keyboard and flat panel display explores the "purpose" of products using visual narrative as a primary tool. The simile of paper (display housing), pencil (adjustable stand) and notebook (the keyboard) is used to visually narrate the writing, collecting and retrieval of information. These images of familiar objects can be "metaphorically" read at different levels by a variety of cultural groups.

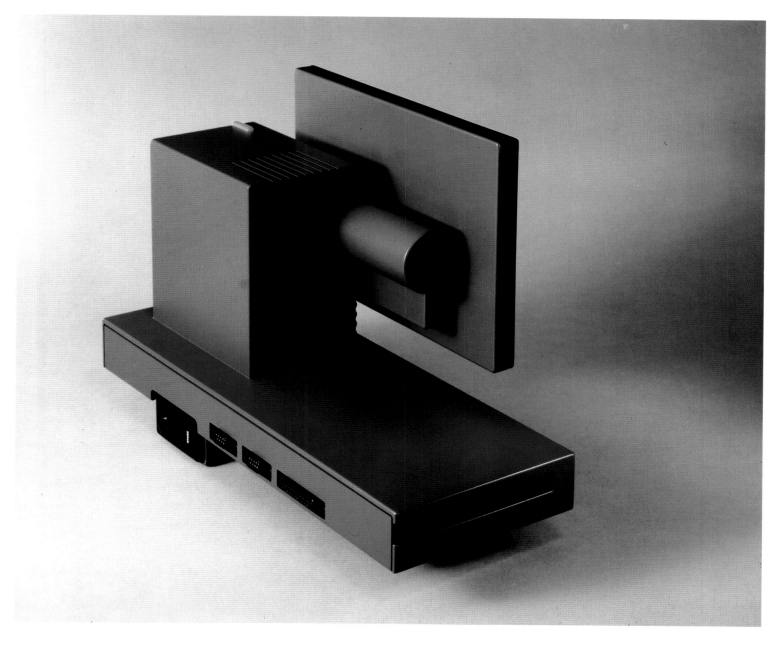

PRODUCT
LANstation II
DESIGNERS
Sohrab Vossoughi, Paul Furner,
David Knaub
DESIGN FIRM
Ziba Design
CLIENT/MFR
Emerald Computers
AWARD
Silver 1989

The LANstation II is a full-function diskless, IBM-compatible PC used as a local area network terminal. Its compact design was achieved with the use of a thin, electro-luminescent screen instead of a CRT. Its configuration facilitates cooling by natural convection, eliminating the need for a bulky fan.

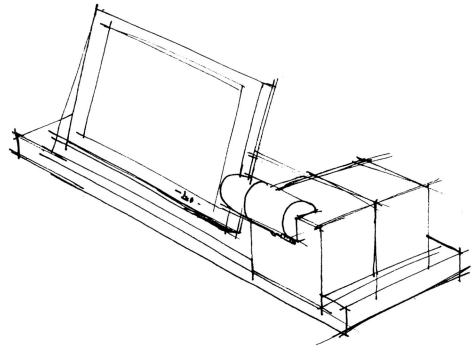

PRODUCT
"Swyft" Personal Computer
DESIGNER
Jonathan Burke
DESIGN FIRM
Argyle Design
CLIENT/MFR
Information Appliance
AWARD
Bronze 1989

A diskless laptop computer, the Swyft is intended to act as an idea processing platform for a variety of users. Its wordprocessing program is designed to be as easy to use as a traditional typewriter. In addition, it features a built-in modem as well as a spreadsheet program and calculator. Its minimal size requires little space in a briefcase or backpack.

PRODUCT
Business Computer
DESIGNER
Ching-Liang Wang while a student at Cranbrook Academy of Art
AWARD
Silver 1988

This computer encourages maximum interaction between two or more people at a single terminal and is especially appropriate for use in banking, real estate or automobile showroom transactions. In a bank, for example, the Business Computer makes it possible for both parties to take part in financial discussions via the terminal screen.

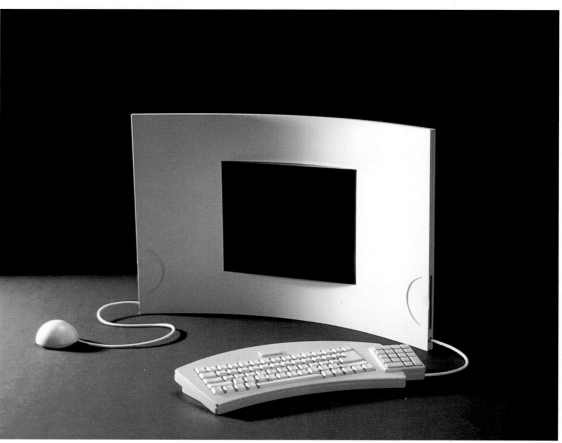

PRODUCT
InFocus PC Viewer 6448C,
6448C + 2
DESIGNERS
Sohrab Vossoughi, Christopher Alviar,
Terry Jones
DESIGN FIRM
Ziba Design
CLIENT/MFR
InFocus Systems, Inc.
AWARD
Silver 1988

An electronic visual presentation tool, the PC Viewer is intended for use by business executives, salespeople and teachers. The user connects the Viewer to a personal computer, places the Viewer on an overhead projector and is then ready to present any image shown or generated on the computer. A remote control unit and separate memory module are available as optional equipment.

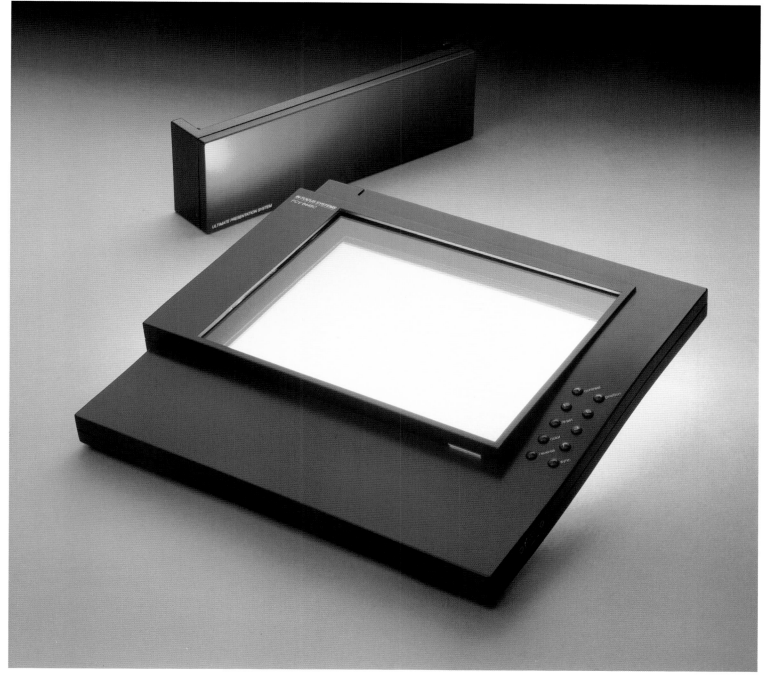

PRODUCT
VUE 2.0 Visual User Environment
DESIGNERS
Barry Mathis, Steve Anderson,
Shiz Kobara
DESIGN FIRM
Hewlett Packard
CLIENT/MFR
Hewlett Packard Interface Technology
Operation
AWARD
Gold 1990

This product has expanded the role of industrial design from the computer hardware to the computer screen itself. VUE is a strikingly graphic extension of OSF/Motif, the emerging industry standard user interface for UNIX computers. All of VUE's capability is visually and functionally focused in a dashboard-like panel across the bottom of the screen, giving the user constant access to all of the controls and functions needed in the UNIX environment.

PRODUCT
SPC
DESIGNERS
Lawrence Lam, Michael Nuttall
DESIGN FIRM
Matrix Product Design, Inc.
CLIENT/MFR
Convergent Technologies
AWARD
Silver 1988

The SPC functions as the main computer in a small business or as an inter-departmental computer within a large company. Because it is likely to be placed in the middle of a room, every side of the SPC is designed to be aesthetically pleasing. A door covers the drives and user controls at the front. Another door on the side covers bulky connectors, eliminating a "hardware look" and allowing the SPC to blend into the office environment.

PRODUCT
Cogent Research XTM Workstation
DESIGNER
Larry Vollum
DESIGN FIRM
Vollum Design
CLIENT/MFR
Cogent Research
AWARD
Bronze 1989

The Cogent Research XTM Workstation was the first of a new generation of desktop super-computers. The design needed to befit the XTM's advanced technology yet be affordable to manufacture in low volumes. To this end, the entire enclosure is made of sheet aluminum, including the bezel, allowing a unique and graceful appearance.

PRODUCT
Integrity S2
DESIGNER
Dave Schenone
DESIGN FIRM
Tandem Computers
CLIENT/MFR
Tandem Computers
AWARD
Bronze 1990

The S2 is a multi-user, fault-tolerant UNIX-based expand-able computer. Ergonomically designed, all internal compo-nents are color-coded and la-beled to enhance simplicity of use. The result is lower maintenance costs. More-over, the product can be ser-viced by a disabled end user.

PRODUCT
6386E WGS Processor
DESIGNERS
Stephen Miggels, Henry Mack,
Daniel Harden
DESIGN FIRM
Henry Dreyfuss Associates
CLIENT/MFR
AT&T
AWARD
Bronze 1989

This computer is intended for use by residential consumers or small businesses and can accommodate disks for up to 300 million characters. The design problem was to redesign a vendor's product to fit into the AT&T product family in terms of overall look, visual icons, and human factor interaction. The front bezel and control panel were redesigned and a handle was added, enabling the user to pull the unit out from under a desk.

PRODUCT
Tsunami
DESIGNERS
Sohrab Vossoughi, Tom Froning,
Henry Chin
DESIGN FIRM
Ziba Design
CLIENT/MFR
La Cie Ltd.
AWARD
Bronze 1990

An add-on hard disk drive
for Apple's Macintosh computers, the Tsunami is innovative in its size and
detailing. Every detail is
functional, providing stability, modularity and visual interest. The cylinder creates
an "air space" to reduce operating noise and improve
airflow.

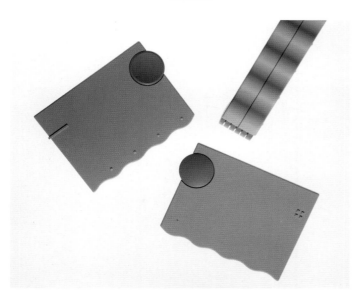

PRODUCT
3 Server
DESIGNERS
Robert Brunner, Max Yoshimoto
DESIGN FIRM
Lunar Design
CLIENT/MFR
3 Com Corp.
AWARD
Bronze 1989

The 3 Server is a desktop file serving device for use in conjunction with 3 Com's family of networking software and hardware products in an office environment. It allows many users to share the same file system from their personal computers or workstations and requires minimum interaction with the user.

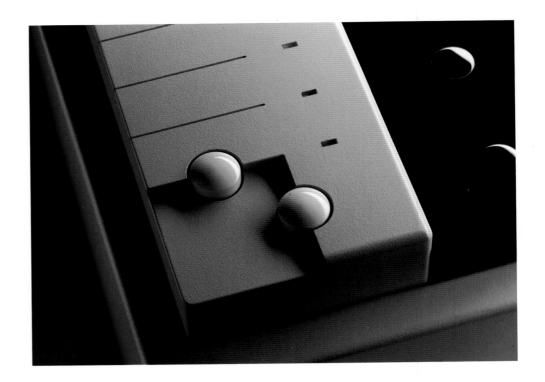

PRODUCT
Sigma Non-Impact Printer
DESIGNERS
Barbara K. Lewis, John Jamieson
DESIGN FIRMS
Barbara Lewis, Industrial Design;
Design Werks!
CLIENT/MFR
Qume Corp.
AWARD
Gold 1988

The Sigma Non-Impact Printer is intended for use by anyone who requires printing flexibility, such as desktop publishers. It is small, quiet, quick, reasonably priced, letter quality and has graphics capabilities. The design makes all functions obvious: the small buttons are to pause or restart the printing process, and to advance the paper; the power button was moved from the back to the top where it is easily accessible, but not easily turned off.

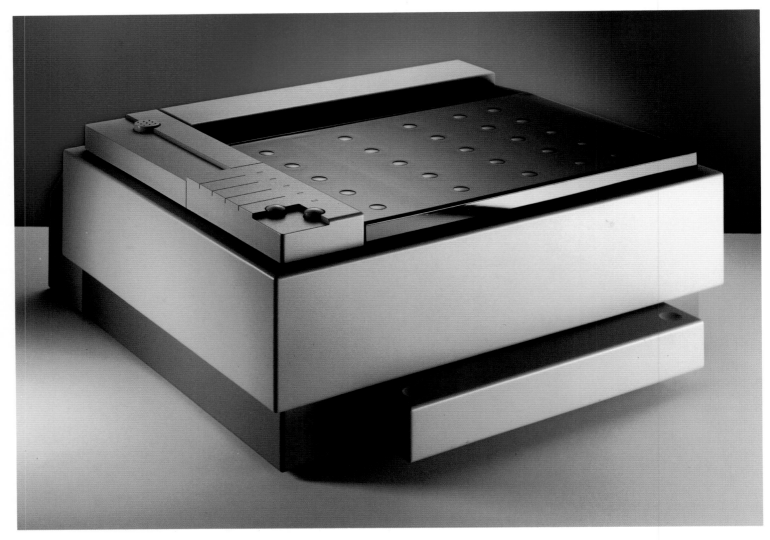

PRODUCT
Mouse
DESIGNERS
Paul Bradley, Michael Nuttall
DESIGN FIRM
Matrix Product Design, Inc.
CLIENT/MFR
Microsoft
AWARD
Silver 1988

This product reflects several changes in the standard mouse design. The Microsoft Mouse was designed with the ball in the front so that a minimal amount of wrist action gives the maximum amount of movement on the monitor. The left button (used 95 percent of the time) was made larger than the right, which was found to benefit both right and left-handed users.

PRODUCT
Freestyle Full-Page Tablet and Stylus
DESIGNERS
Thom Tedham, Douglas Dayton
DESIGN FIRM
Wang Laboratories, Inc.
CLIENT/MFR
Wang Laboratories, Inc.
AWARD
Bronze 1989

This product allows the user to imprint a screenful of information with questions, comments or directives written by their own hand and spoken in their own voice. The Input Tablet and Stylus provide all but the speech function, which is handled by a special handset.

PRODUCT
Terminal Concentrator
DESIGNERS
Khodi Feiz, Harold Wood,
Bob Wendling
DESIGN FIRM
Texas Instruments
Digital Systems Group
CLIENT/MFR
Texas Instruments
AWARD
Bronze 1989

The Terminal Concentrator
is a unit which concentrates
up to eight terminals into a
mainframe host to eliminate
excessive cabling and en-
hance processing power.
Instead of 64 cables con-
verging into one mainframe,
there are eight terminal con-
centrators interfacing with
the host, each capable of
handling up to eight terminals, effectively reducing the
amount of cabling and simplifying the system.

PRODUCT
Access Floor Workstation Module
DESIGNER
Alan Brownlie
DESIGN FIRM
Brownlie Design Inc.
CLIENT/MFR
AMP Inc
AWARD
Silver 1990

This module allows the user
to readily access and recon-
figure power, data and communication services, a
critical advantage in the
ever-changing environment
of the information-intensive
workplace. By making electri-
cal outlets integral with the
cover, services can be viewed
and easily accessed when the
unit is opened. Once the
power and data cords are
plugged in, the cover is
closed with the wires routed
through a protective shield
which goes into place
automatically.

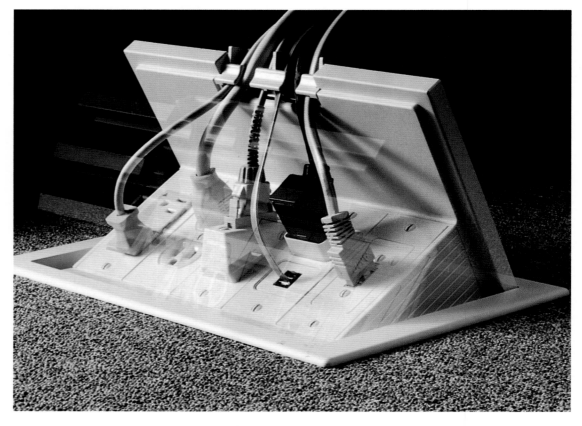

PRODUCT
DataMyte 9000
DESIGNERS
Daniel Cunagin, Eric Mueller,
Eugene Reshanov
DESIGN FIRM
Polivka Logan Designers, Inc.
CLIENT/MFR
DataMyte Corp.
AWARD
Silver 1989

The DataMyte 9000 is a portable data collection device for statistical process control. It is used in quality control, manufacturing, engineering and laboratory testing. Its rugged enclosure can withstand an industrial environment and has secure and comfortable grips for a gloved hand.

PRODUCT
VICOM Set
DESIGNER
Eric P. Chan
DESIGN FIRM
Ecco Inc.
CLIENT/MFR
NYNEX
AWARD
Bronze 1990

This prototype is an integrated voice-image communications station system which incorporates many unique features in a compact package. It includes an interactive display, a printer, an onscreen keyboard, a speakerphone and a writing pad. A light-colored section defines the basic and frequently used telephone operations.

PRODUCT
7766 Proof Workstation
DESIGN FIRM
NCR Design Staff
CLIENT/MFR
NCR Corp.
AWARD
Bronze 1990

This banking product is used to encode and endorse checks or other documents so that they can be machine read during further processing within the banking system. The design improves productivity while providing a comfortable and safe working posture for extended periods of use.

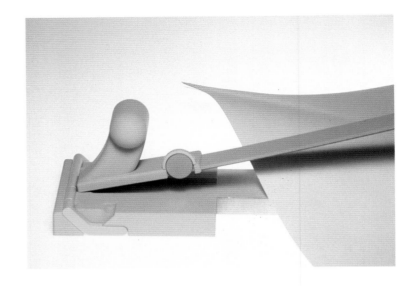

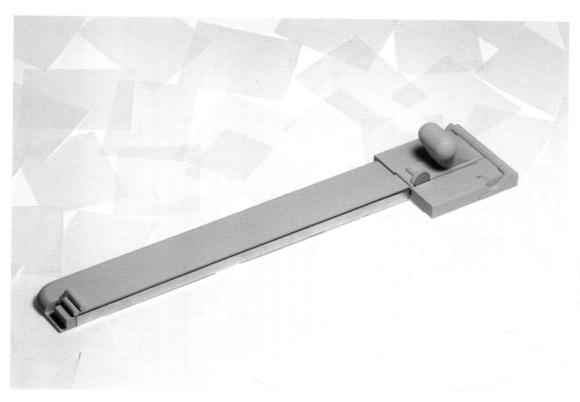

PRODUCT
Paper Cutter
DESIGNER
Glenn Polinsky
AWARD
Silver 1988

To use this papercutter, one lifts the yellow horizontal bar, slides the paper under, pulls up the yellow tab to lock the bar in place and then pushes the handle forward causing the circular blade to rotate and cut the paper. The rolling blade was put out in front of the handle for high visibility and covered with a shield to protect the user's hands.

PRODUCT
Quorum Microphone/Loudspeaker
DESIGNERS
Gordon Sylvester, Daniel Harden
DESIGN FIRM
Henry Dreyfuss Associates
CLIENT/MFR
AT&T
AWARD
Bronze 1989

The Quorum is an innovative microphone/loudspeaker that provides highly sensitive speech pickup for large conferences in a business setting. Twenty-eight omni-directional microphones are housed in an aluminum pole that fits into a pyramidal base containing the speaker and circuit board.

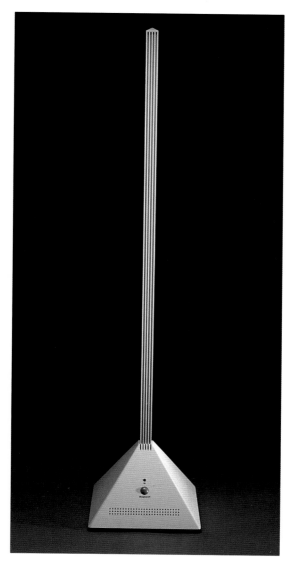

CHAPTER 5

FURNITURE
AND
FIXTURES

NEWHOUSE GROUP™ FURNITURE

"This extensive system of modular furniture is an excellent expression of Industrial Design where a mass produced, highly tooled product line achieves the essentials of solving a broad range of user's needs and meets many of the manufacturer's objectives. It represents an innovative combination of pleasing aesthetics, ergonomic resolution and product functionality."

—*Juror* **Jack Kelley**

PERCEPTION STACKING CHAIR

"In both form and function, this chair provides a striking alternative to traditional offerings in this market. We were impressed by the use of materials and the options that provide for use and storage."

—*Juror* **Patricia Moore**, IDSA

CONTEXT™

"This system offers a solution that breaks away!"

—*Juror* **Brian Kane**, IDSA

PRODUCT
Context™
DESIGNER
Terry West
DESIGN FIRM
Steelcase Environmental
Systems Design Group
CLIENT/MFR
Steelcase Inc.
AWARD
Gold 1989

This adaptable, freestanding furniture system can be combined in different ways to meet varied functional, environmental and aesthetic conditions. Choices in workstation configuration, privacy/interaction needs and visual details make the system suitable for a wide range of information workers, from support staff to management.

PRODUCT
Newhouse Group™ Furniture
DESIGNER
Thomas J. Newhouse
DESIGN FIRM
Thomas J. Newhouse Design
CLIENT/MFR
Herman Miller, Inc.
AWARD
Gold 1988

This furniture system provides a comprehensive, modular and affordable free-standing desk and storage range that can support the constantly evolving work process needs of a broad range of office workers. It is designed to support both manual and automated work—writing, filing, computing, etc. All pieces are detailed for exceptional user comfort.

PRODUCT
Ethospace Support Cabinets
DESIGNERS
Jean Beirise and Geoff Hollington
in collaboration with
Herman Miller Design
DESIGN FIRMS
Coons & Beirise Design, Inc.;
Hollington Associates
CLIENT/MFR
Herman Miller, Inc.
AWARD
Silver 1989

As enhancements to the Ethospace system, these support cabinets can be either freestanding or integrated structurally with Ethospace walls. When integrated, they can eliminate the need for return walls, connectors and finishing hardware. Their consolidated storage means that system wall heights are not dictated by storage needs.

PRODUCT
'Next' Chair Program
DESIGNER
Richard Penney
DESIGN FIRM
The Richard Penney
Design Group, Inc.
CLIENT/MFR
Interna Designs, Ltd.
AWARD
Bronze 1989

'Next' is a modular chair program designed to respond to many different residential and contract possibilities. The innovative back has a small amount of flex, along with an anthropomorphic contour which provides comfort and support not usually found in wood chairs. Available in a variety of forms, colors and finishes, 'Next' offers a broad spectrum of design options suitable for a wide variety of users.

PRODUCT
Perception Stacking Chair
DESIGNERS
Warren H. Snodgrass, Charles Roth
DESIGN FIRM
Design Technology
CLIENT/MFR
Tropitone Furniture Co.
AWARD
Gold 1990

This rugged, all-weather chair can be left outside year round. It features an ergonomically designed seat and back, formed from perforated aluminum sheet and supported by a frame of rectangular aluminum tube. The relationship between the arm and rear leg allows the chairs to stack for easy storage.

PRODUCT
Corvo Chair
DESIGNERS
Orlando Diaz-Aczuy, Zooey Chu
DESIGN FIRM
Orlando Diaz-Aczuy Associates
CLIENT/MFR
Steelcase Inc.
AWARD
Bronze 1989

An occasional guest chair for office use, the Corvo is a mid-priced chair line available in both arm and armless models. Constructed of tubular steel welded together in pairs, the chair is both strong and visually innovative.

PRODUCT
700–704 Manhattan Collection
DESIGNER
Brian Kane
DESIGN FIRM
Metropolitan Furniture Corporation
CLIENT/MFR
Metropolitan Furniture Corporation
AWARD
Gold 1988

This seating collection was developed to provide a side chair solution that would work in a variety of applications, from pull-up to waiting area seating. The innovation of the design lies in the five unique frame solutions available in the chairs and loveseats; each frame shares common design elements, yet each has a special arm and back detailing. The relatively small scale of this collection makes it ideal for use in limited spaces.

PRODUCT
Parade! Stacking Chair
DESIGNER
Robert M. Scheper
DESIGN FIRM
Steelcase Seating Industrial
Design Group
CLIENT/MFR
Steelcase Inc.
AWARD
Silver 1989

Parade is a stacking chair to be used in auditoriums, conference areas and cafeterias, as well as an occasional chair in offices. Superior comfort, increased support area and improved seating contours were achieved by innovatively configuring wire frame to the shell of the seat.

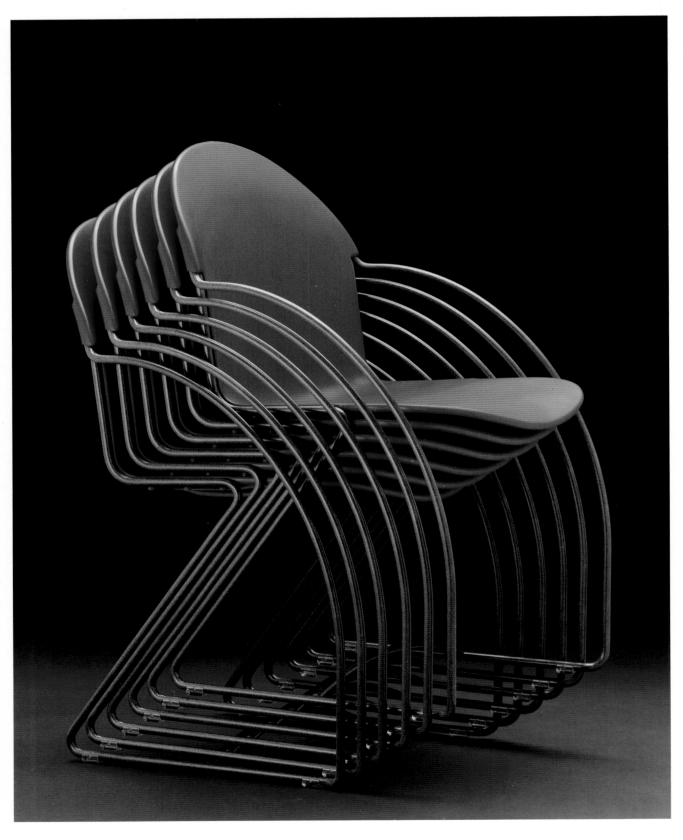

PRODUCT
Pacifica Lounge and Side Chair
DESIGNER
Brian Kane
DESIGN FIRM
Kane Design Studio
CLIENT/MFR
Metropolitan Furniture Corp.
AWARD
Silver 1990

This collection of lounge, loveseat, sofa and side chair features aesthetic and functional details that bridge both contract and residential needs. Fine upholstery detailing and traditional wood craftsmanship contribute to the elegance of its design.

PRODUCT
Carousel Exterior Table and Seats
DESIGNER
Arno York
DESIGN FIRM
LFI
CLIENT/MFR
LFI
AWARD
Bronze 1990

The Carousel provides vandal resistant exterior dining in corporate and university settings. Simple, straightforward yet unique, the Carousel is a one-piece table and seating unit. The table top is available in either fiberglass or metal and the attached seats are either wire or perforated metal.

PRODUCT
Utility Table Collection
DESIGNER
Niels Diffrient
CLIENT/MFR
Howe Furniture Corporation
AWARD
Silver 1989

Utility tables are used every-
where from executive suites
to cafeterias, from training
rooms to conference rooms.
The design for this collection
gives special attention to
user involvement, providing
self-evident mechanical ac-
tions for folding, tilting and
attaching legs. All opera-
tional elements were carefully designed and tested to
provide maximum simplicity
of use and absence of user
stress.

PRODUCT
The Sardine Light
DESIGNERS
Tucker Viemeister, Lisa Krohn
CLIENT/MFR
Gallery 91
AWARD
Bronze 1989

A decorative hanging lamp for both adults and children, the Sardine Light utilizes zoomorphic forms to achieve a literary statement. The sardine's silhouette can be viewed as a cartoon, or the fish can be understood in its ancient religious and sexual symbolic context. Beyond its functional role as a lamp, the Sardine Light offers a unique design that affirms diversity and range of choice.

PRODUCT
Lectern
DESIGNER
Winn Whitman Weiner while a student at the University of Texas
AWARD
Bronze 1990

This lectern was designed to reflect the philosophy of the Unity faith. It mounts on the pulpit of a Unity Church without acting as a barrier between the minister and congregation, and it incorporates both a cross and a wing, symbols of the Unity faith. Unlike traditional podiums, this design rises up off a single column with a cross-shaped void in its center.

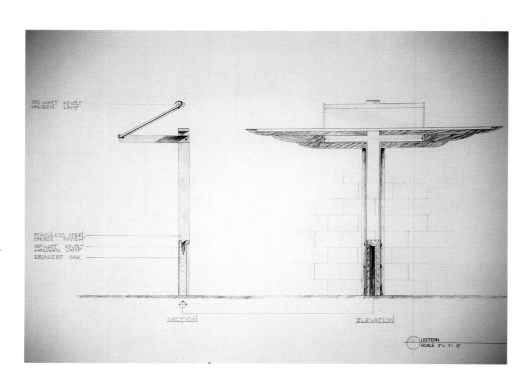

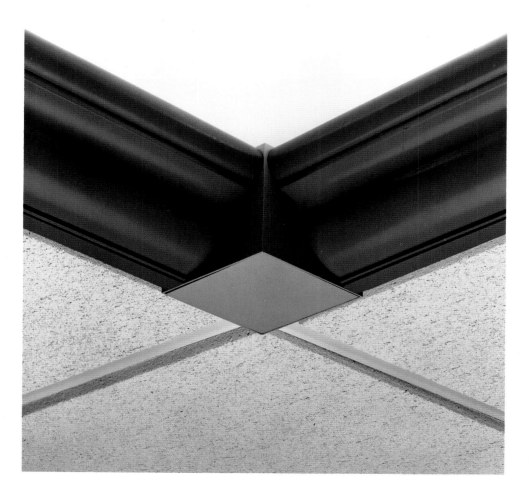

PRODUCT
Beamers™
DESIGNERS
James B. Libby, Patrick M. Brown
DESIGN FIRM
Winona Lighting Studio, Inc.
CLIENT/MFR
Winona Lighting
AWARD
Silver 1988

Beamers™ is an innovative modular lighting system intended for use with suspended ceiling systems. It enables users to create a unique ceiling, introducing color, pattern and flexibility within a very efficient lighting system. Three molding options—Stepped, Classic and Quarter Round—are available, along with 13 lacquered and 3 anodized metallic finishes.

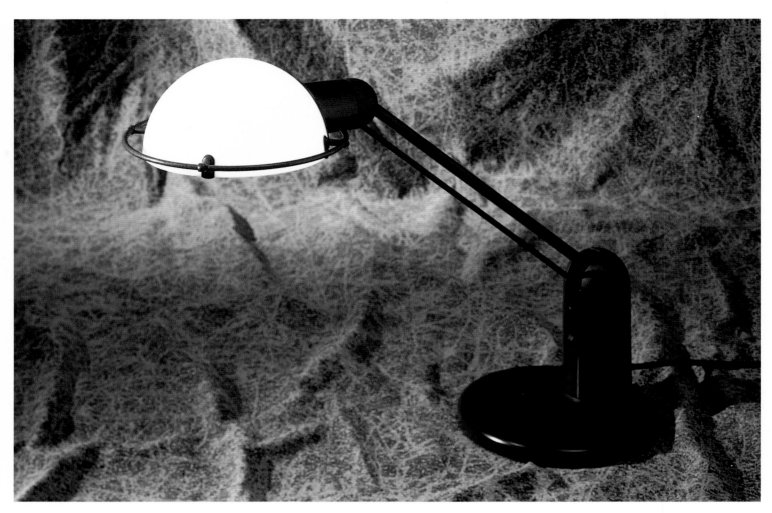

PRODUCT
Lyra Lamp
DESIGNER
Terence Duncan
DESIGN FIRM
Steelcase Industrial Design
CLIENT/MFR
Steelcase, Inc.
AWARD
Bronze 1989

The Lyra Lamp provides portable task lighting in (but not exclusive to) the CONTEXT™ freestanding system furniture. The dome has a limited pivot of 30 degrees, blocking direct light to the user's eyes without annoying someone sitting across from the lamp. Freestanding or mounted, the Lyra Lamp fits visually and functionally with all the environments sold by Steelcase, Inc.

PRODUCT
W.A.V.E. Illuminated Magnifier Lamp
DESIGNERS
Mark Steiner, Paul Mulhauser, Douglas Spranger
DESIGN FIRM
Human Factors/Industrial Design, Inc.
CLIENT/MFR
Luxo Lamp Corp.
AWARD
Silver 1989

This illuminated magnifying lamp is suitable for inspecting electronic circuit boards. By studying the specific needs of users, the designers developed a large, field-of-view lens with lighting appropriate for inspection tasks. This magnifier head provides about 13 inches of horizontal field-of-view, representing an increase of 53 percent over conventional round magnifiers.

PRODUCT
Pan a Lux Indirect Lighting Fixtures
DESIGNER
Douglas M. Green
CLIENT/MFR
Rambusch Company
AWARD
Bronze 1989

Pan a Lux is a line of indirect lighting fixtures using reflector designs that Rambusch had previously developed for architectural lighting instruments. Three reflector shapes engineered almost 20 years ago were transformed into architectural lighting fixtures that can be appreciated for their unique function as well as their appearance. The form of each fixture expresses the shape of its reflector and the light it distributes.

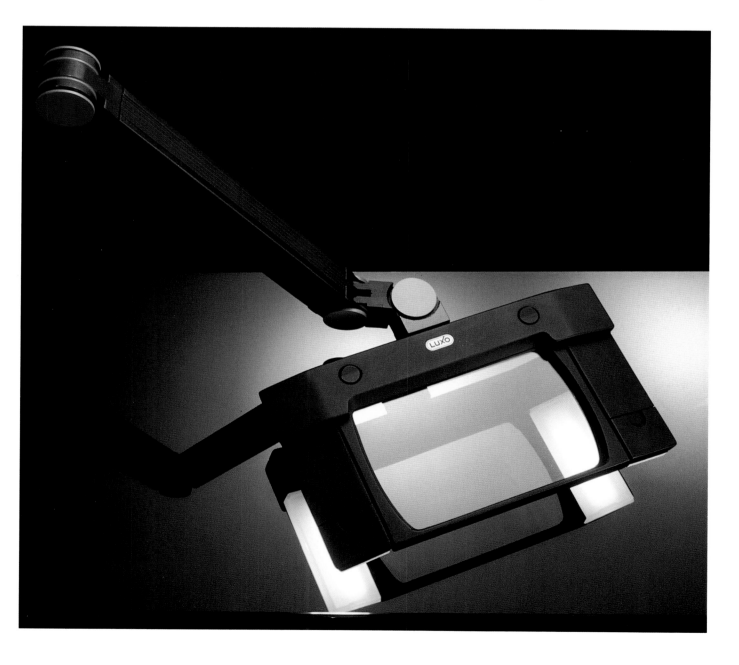

PRODUCT
Luméa Designer Lighting Controls
and Accessories
DESIGNERS
Elliot Jacoby, Darryl Tucker,
Wayne Kahn, Noel Mayo
DESIGN FIRM
Lutron Electronics Company, Inc.
CLIENT/MFR
Lutron Electronics Company, Inc.
AWARD
Bronze 1989

Luméa Designer Lighting
Controls and Accessories
provide a unique, clean,
contemporary design with
superior lighting control
performance. They can be
roughed in during building
construction, enabling the
consumer to select faceplate
colors later when decorating.
An innovative feature of this
system is that faceplates and
inserts can be removed to
change the color when decor
changes.

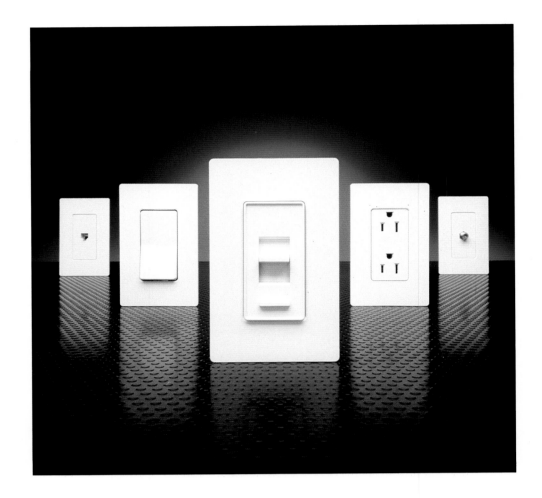

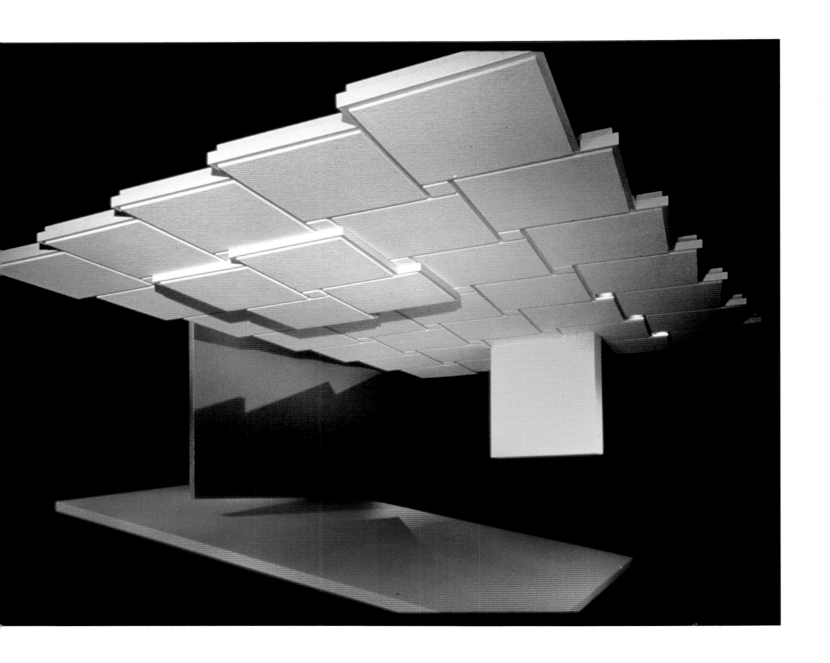

PRODUCT
Intersections Ceiling System
DESIGNERS
David T. Mieyal, Robert J. Surra,
Paul Lalonde
DESIGN FIRM
U.S.G. Interiors, Inc.
CLIENT/MFR
U.S.G. Interiors, Inc.
AWARD
Bronze 1990

This system is a technically elegant structure which starts with a single suspension element, installed at angles to create a range of design options. It is the first "ashlar" or "basket weave" grid system to pass seismic pullout tests. While allowing a deconstructivist look, its details make it compatible with various room shapes.

C H A P T E R 6

ENVIRONMENTAL DESIGN

TINO COSMA/ELLEGI SHOWROOM

"This design shows an intelligent application of cost- and time-saving techniques that piqued the jury's enthusiasm. Overall, it presents a contemporary image without resorting to cliche."

—*Juror* **Clyde Foles,** IDSA

PROJECT
Echo Showroom-New York
DESIGNERS
Bruce Burdick, Susan Kosakowsky
Burdick, Bruce Lightbody
DESIGN FIRM
The Burdick Group
CLIENT/MFR
The Echo Design Group
AWARD
1990 Silver

The design for this show-room is both intimate and intelligent, a place where buyers want to go and where salespeople can physically present the product line of more than 400 scarves and 100 belts efficiently and rapidly. The solution focuses on a centrally located pavilion housing a scarf library, from which scarves can be accessed and presented. Scarf display holes were designed out of steel, plastic and rubber, allowing scarves to be draped from walls and easily changed.

PROJECT
Tino Cosma/Ellegi Showroom
DESIGNERS
Eric Rosenberg, Michele Kolb
DESIGN FIRM
Eric Rosenberg, Architect with
Michele Kolb Design
CLIENT/MFR
Tino Cosma, Inc./Ellegi, Inc.
AWARD
Gold 1989

The New York showrooms for
Tino Cosma, Inc., a men's
neckwear manufacturer, and
Ellegi, Inc., a women's ap-
parel line, are designed as
flexible spaces with a loft-
like sense of openness. A
neutral shell provides an appropriate backdrop for the
clothing lines. The architectural image was conceived
to reflect each company's
clothing, their mutual association and their individual
distinctions.

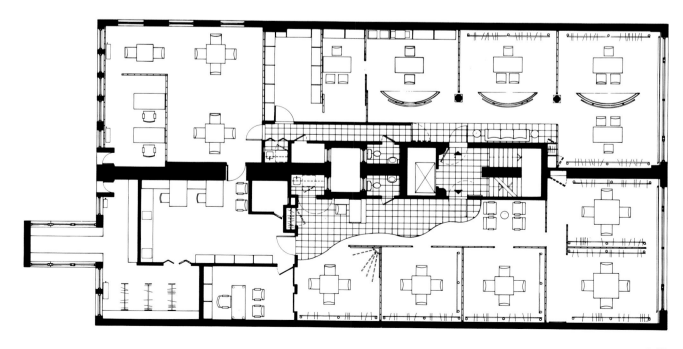

PROJECT
Atelier International (AI) Ltd.
DESIGNERS
Richard Penney, Erica Pritchard,
Frank Young
DESIGN FIRM
The Richard Penney Group
CLIENT/MFR
Atelier International Ltd.
AWARD
Bronze 1990

This showroom was designed to be a flexible architectural stage which could change as the company evolves. The showroom and offices are a fusion of classic and modern design. The expansive show windows, penetrated by two deep glass entryways set at 45-degree angles to the public corridors, provide an invitation to enter and window-shop.

PROJECT
Southland Food Fair, Southland Mall
DESIGNER
Tony Horton
DESIGN FIRM
T L Horton Design, Inc.
CLIENT/MFR
Equity Properties & Development
Company
AWARD
Bronze 1989

This budget-sensitive reno-
vation created an exciting,
colorful environment for
shoppers to rest, enjoy entertainment and eat. Brightly
colored arched entries with
the logo i.d. and neon lit directional signage were created to be highly visible
down mall corridors. Addi-
tional planters were added
to the atrium food court,
along with festive umbrellas
and banners.

PROJECT
The Solutions Center
DESIGNERS
Merritt W. Seymour, Robert J. Surra,
Merle Lindby-Young
DESIGN FIRM
USG Interiors, Inc.
CLIENT/MFR
USG Interiors, Inc.
AWARD
Silver 1990

The Solutions Center, Chicago, is a 13,000 square foot loft space used for product display, product mock-ups, industrial design and presentations for USG Interiors, Inc. Chicago common brick and timber, the original building materials, were retained to create a background for modern, prefinished interior products.

PROJECT
Save Rite Jewelry Store
DESIGNERS
Peter Wooding, Rolando Moreno,
Chiara Van Erp
DESIGN FIRM
Peter Wooding Design Associates
CLIENT/MFR
Save Rite Jewelry Store
AWARD
Silver 1988

This project developed a totally new design and image for a discount jewelry store to make it compatible with a prestigious location in a high-rise office building. It required fitting the store's merchandise into two and one-half times less space. Wall displays were designed and used to increase merchandise density; accent light columns were designed to provide relief and avoid a cluttered look.

PROJECT
Union
DESIGNER
James Geier
DESIGN FIRM
555 Design Fabrication Management
Inc.
CLIENT/MFR
Union
AWARD
Silver 1989

The interior design for this progressive, upscale nightclub utilizes a unique mix of materials, finishes and lighting to create a visually interesting, textural space while maintaining an intimate residential feeling. Lighting is soft but dramatic when playing off a variety of patterned metal work. Exposed brick walls serve as an interesting backdrop to strategically placed lighting, video monitors and artwork.

PROJECT
Video Concepts
DESIGN FIRM
Design Forum, Inc.
CLIENT/MFR
Tandy NBRG
AWARD
Bronze 1990

This store environment features a spacious entrance area that showcases the latest in personal electronics. The products are easy to see against the sleek displays of dazzling white accented with red and black. Angled wall units throughout coax customers to investigate the entire store and help define the various product categories.

PRODUCT
Newspaper Dispenser
DESIGNER
Beth Mosher while a student at the University of Illinois
AWARD
Silver 1990

This concept for a newspaper dispenser grew out of an exploration of the nature of streets and the way in which they both contain and result from our activity. The angled container gradually lowers as each paper is removed while allowing the remaining papers to be easily viewed. The natural finishes of the metal allow the handles to be polished where they are frequently touched, providing a cue for future customers.

PROJECT
Amoco Station of the Future
DESIGNERS
Selame Design Group
DESIGN FIRM
Selame Design
CLIENT/MFR
Amoco Oil Company
AWARD
Gold 1988

This state-of-the-art Amoco service station is designed to be compatible with the company's image standards and with today's technology. It also provides for future changes. It incorporates features to speed transactions, improve security and safety for employees and customers, ease driveway/pump congestion and give a unique, updated look distinct from all competition.

C H A P T E R **7**

EXHIBITS AND COMMUNICATION GRAPHICS

INVISIBLE FORCES

"This is a beautiful example of an interactive, participatory exhibit. It is truly hands-on and engages the audience through active participation. Moreover, it looks like its subject—honest, direct and durable."

—*Juror* **Louis Nelson,** IDSA

ROBES OF ELEGANCE

"This design is masterfully done in its solution of difficult problems while letting the objects exhibited remain the primary focal point. The spacial organization of the exhibit is elegantly simple."

—*Juror* **Gianfranco Zaccai,** IDSA

SITEGUIDE™

"SITEGUIDE's appearance fits the environment. It uses electronic technology very well by giving visual and hard copy for the visitor's convenience."

—*Juror* **Louis Nelson,** IDSA

PROJECT
Robes of Elegance: Japanese Kimonos
of the 16th–20th Centuries
DESIGNERS
Lida Lowrey, Kerry Boyd,
Jennie Malcolm
DESIGN FIRM
North Carolina Museum of Art
CLIENT/MFR
North Carolina Museum of Art
AWARD
Gold 1989

The basic objective of this exhibition was to convey the beauty and history of the art of Japan. Due to the fragile nature of the centuries-old kimonos, rigorous temperature, humidity and light controls were paramount. No screws, nails or metal of any kind were allowed in the case interiors, for fear of snagging the garments. The kimono stands were constructed out of unfinished white oak using traditional Japanese joinery methods.

PROJECT
WestWeek 1987 Exhibition
DESIGNER
Robert Arko
DESIGN FIRM
Metropolitan Furniture Corporation
CLIENT/MFR
Metropolitan Furniture Corporation
AWARD
Gold 1988

The intent of this design was to provide a temporary, provocative environment for a contract furniture manufacturer product display during a major industry market. The designer used spun polyester as a material boundary because the material reflected colored light and remained transparent so that the furniture could be seen from outside as well as from within the room.

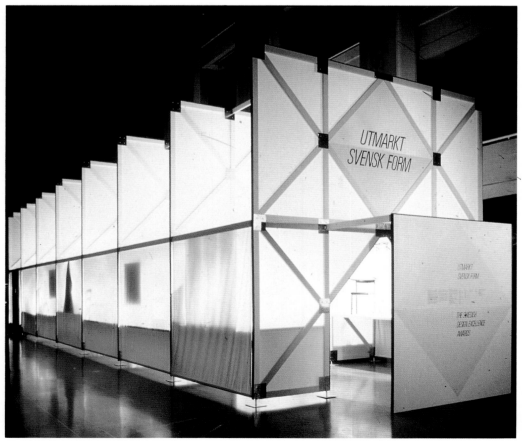

PROJECT
The Swedish National Product Design Awards Traveling Exhibit
DESIGNERS
Harvey Bernstein, Lukie Kornbluth, Lori A. Miner
DESIGN FIRM
Bernstein Design Associates
CLIENT/MFR
Childesign
AWARD
Silver 1990

This flexible exhibit showed small-scale products in a scaled-down space that could expand or contract depending on the size of the venue. Easy to set up and ship, the exhibit used only off-the-shelf components, fixtures and materials. Airy and pleasant to walk through, the tensile space-frame exhibit system made an appropriate display environment for the Swedish products.

PROJECT
KI Merchandise Mart Showroom/
The Piretti Collection
DESIGNER
Massimo Vignelli
DESIGN FIRM
Vignelli & Associates
CLIENT/MFR
KI
AWARD
Silver 1989

This trade show in Chicago's Merchandise Mart focused on an extensive new line of seating that presented a fresh concept of ergonomic design. Opting for a theatrical effect, the showroom designer created a display that spanned the entire width of the room. Chairs were upholstered in bright red and placed on a low stage backed by a graphic presentation of the designer along with an explanation of the new seating concept. The inviting display encouraged visitors to test the product.

PROJECT
TRIAD Design Project
DESIGNERS
Chris Pullman, Alison Kennedy,
Douglas Scott, Dr. Karen Freeze,
Earl Powell, Jane Corbus
DESIGN FIRMS
WGBH/Boston; Design Management
Institute; Giltspur Exhibits
CLIENT/MFR
Design Management Institute
AWARD
Silver 1990

This traveling exhibition illustrates how 13 companies worldwide have creatively and effectively managed design. It is an outgrowth of the TRIAD Design Project, an international research program which explores the role of design management as a key aspect of competitive strategy. The exhibition displays nine stages in the product development process and shows design as an on-going process that is involved in every aspect of a product's development.

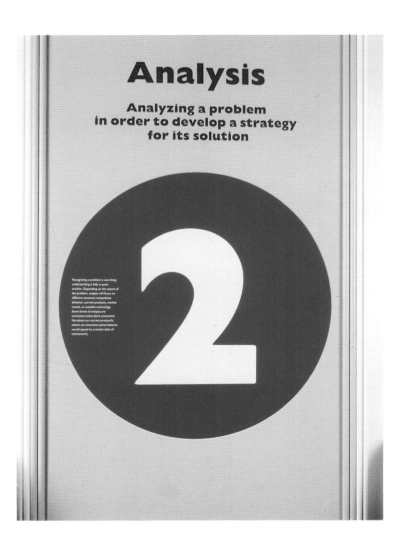

PROJECT
The Fine Art of American
Industrial Design
DESIGNERS
Tucker Viemeister, Martha Davis,
Steve Russak, Tom Dair,
Tamara Thomsen, Virginia Edwards,
Douglas Green, Mark Walhimes,
Danielle Deluliis, Paul Mulhauser
DESIGN FIRM
Smart Design, Inc.
DESIGN CURATORS:
Rheda Brandt, David Gallager, Richard
Schmidt, Lorenzo Porcelli, Tucker
Viemeister
CLIENT/MFR
National Arts Club
AWARD
Silver 1990

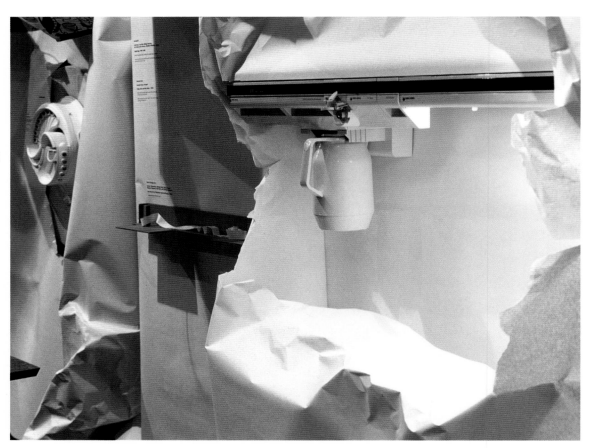

By illustrating the fine art of American design with contemporary examples of automobiles, appliances, furnishings, housewares, toys and scientific apparatus, this exhibit stimulated appreciation for, and a keener understanding of, the work of industrial designers. A ribbon of gleaming white photo backdrop paper separated the exhibit from the drab gallery space. Visitors were encouraged to perceive not only the functional invention of the artifacts, but also to feel the design's artistic expression.

PROJECT
"On the Edge: Industrial Design in
Southern California"
DESIGN FIRM
IDSA/Los Angeles Chapter
CLIENT/MFR
IDSA/Los Angeles Chapter
AWARD
Silver 1990

Opened during WestWeek at
the Pacific Design Center,
this exhibit showcases industrial design to generate
awareness of its scope and
impact for the general public
and to generate coverage of
the topic by area media.
Products were presented
not as museum pieces, but
rather as relatable, consum-
able items found in our lives
every day. The exhibit atmo-
sphere was like an active
warehouse in which products
were being packaged for
shipment across the country.

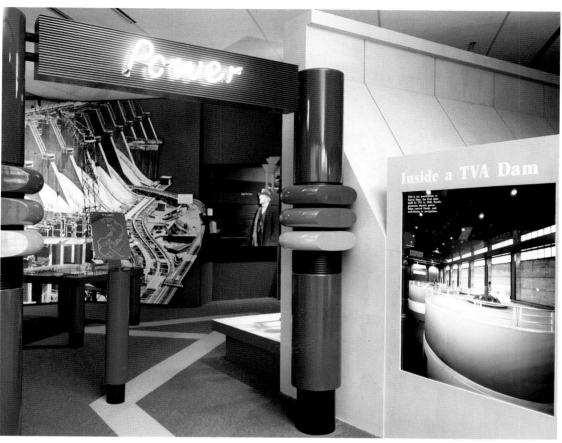

PROJECT
Energy Information Center
DESIGNERS
David Pesanelli, Richard Thomas
DESIGN FIRM
David Pesanelli Associates
CLIENT/MFR
Tennessee Valley Authority
AWARD
Silver 1988

A colorful and somewhat playful information environment, the TVA Energy Information Center is designed to both inform and entertain a broad segment of the general population. Each topic is expressed by several media, including animation, graphics, artifacts, models, video tapes and touch-screen monitors. The project reflects a close collaboration between designers and behavioral scientists.

PROJECT
SciTrek, The Science & Technology
Museum of Atlanta
DESIGNERS
Tim Gilland, Rodger Motiska,
Brendan Cuddihee
DESIGN FIRM
Design/Joe Sondeman, Inc.
CLIENT/MFR
The Science & Technology Museum of
Atlanta
AWARD
Silver 1989

This project required space planning and design of the first phase (20,000 square feet) of exhibits and graphics occupying an existing civic center exhibition hall; all planning, design and production had to be completed within a twelve-month period. The designer developed a modular system for the exhibits consisting of three components: demonstration graphics and base; quick change information/graphic panels; and a simple modular panel exhibit housing enclosure.

PROJECT
Invisible Forces—Electricity and
Magnetism
DESIGNERS
Andrew Kramer, Tim Kobe, Bill Smith,
Lauren Kline, Bonnie Evensen
DESIGN FIRM
West Office Design Associates
CLIENT/MFR
California Museum of Science &
Industry
AWARD
Gold 1990

This exhibition introduces museum visitors to basic concepts of electricity and magnetism utilizing interactive exhibits that allow visitors to learn from experience rather than from explanation. The exhibition imparts specific information, yet it also encourages observation and deduction, the essence of the scientific method. Simple diagrams on exhibit graphic panels make information accessible to visitors from many cultures.

PROJECT
High Rail Bike
DESIGN FIRM
Pacific Science Center Exhibit
Development Group
CLIENT/MFR
Raleigh Bicycle Company, Seattle
Branch
AWARD
Bronze 1989

The High Rail Bike was developed to give the visitor to the Pacific Science Center a kinetic, unforgettable insight into the concept of center of gravity. The bicycle balances on a steel rail 17 feet above the floor and can be ridden by anyone strong enough to pedal a bicycle. A two-hundred pound weight on an eight-foot bar hangs from the bicycle and lowers its center of gravity below the rail.

PROJECT
Baillie Lumber Trade Show Exhibit
DESIGNERS
Jack Snyder, Tim Dexter,
Brian Charters
DESIGN FIRM
Design for Industry, Inc.
CLIENT/MFR
Baillie Lumber Company, Inc.
AWARD
Bronze 1989

This exhibit creates a "glimpse" into a typical Baillie production/distribution facility and places an emphasis on both the Baillie product, native North American hardwoods, and the company's highly qualified people. Solid bundles of various hardwoods against a backdrop of rear-illuminated transparencies suggest an actual scene inside the Baillie Lumber Company.

PROJECT
NASA's Participating Exhibit at the
1989 Paris Air Show
DESIGNERS
Bill Cannan, Tony Ortiz,
H. Kurt Heinz
DESIGN FIRM
Bill Cannan & Co.
CLIENT/MFR
NASA Public Affairs
AWARD
Bronze 1990

This exhibit presented the
complexity and capabilities
of the Hubble Space Tele-
scope to an audience of lay-
men and professionals. It
featured a full-scale cutaway
mock-up of the telescope.
Animated neon rings traced
the path of light entering the
telescope, reflecting off the
primary and secondary mirrors and back to one of five
optical instrument modules
on board.

PROJECT
Watson/Bowman/Acme Trade Show
Exhibit
DESIGNERS
Jack Snyder, Greg Meadows,
Brian Charters
DESIGN FIRM
Design for Industry, Inc.
CLIENT/MFR
Watson/Bowman/Acme
AWARD
Silver 1989

The plan for this exhibit was to develop an impressionistic theatrical setting showing products in their "typical" environment. The overall look was one of concrete, stone or granite, all very common visual references to roadbuilders, bridge builders and architects, but not typically found in a trade show exhibit.

PRODUCT
Multi-Sided Pylon–Non-Illuminated
and Illuminated
DESIGNERS
Ronald W. Cobb, Ben Bell,
Jeff Hampton, Elyse Reeves
DESIGN FIRM
APCO
CLIENT/MFR
APCO
AWARD
Silver 1989

A practical solution to corporate signage and directional identification, the Multi-Sided Pylon modular signage system is designed to provide flexibility, structural integrity and serviceability. The "fastener track" concept allows panels to be moved or removed without modifying the superstructure. The system is easy to ship and assemble and can be installed by two people using a minimum of tools.

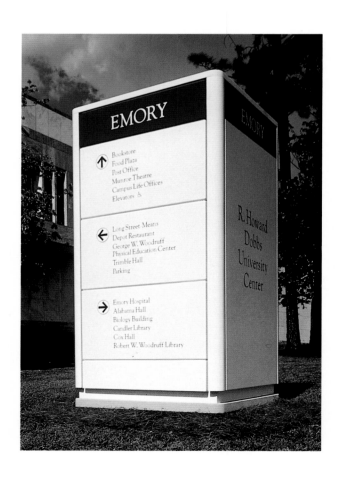

PROJECT
SITEGUIDE™
DESIGNERS
Edwin Schlossberg, John Branigan,
Nancy Hughes
DESIGN FIRM
Edwin Schlossberg, Inc.
CLIENT/MFR
INSIGHTGUIDE PROJECT JOINT
VENTURE
AWARD
Gold 1990

The SITEGUIDE system, installed at the World Financial Center in New York City, is a comprehensive, interactive information and directory system for large, mixed-use real estate developments. Using audio, video, graphics and text, the system provides visitors with directions, easy-to-read maps, descriptions of retail establishments and announcements of events and entertainment programs.

PROJECT
Baltimore Children's Zoo Exhibit
Graphics
DESIGNER
Eileen Tennor
DESIGN FIRM
LDR International, Inc.
CLIENT/MFR
Maryland Zoological Society
AWARD
Silver 1990

The exhibit graphics of the Children's Zoo enhance the learning experience, communicating important and often complex ideas and ecological facts in the most direct way possible. With a simple vocabulary and an emphasis on pictures, the exhibits communicate to very young children while keeping the focus on the animals and the naturalistic environment created to showcase each ecosystem of the story line.

175

PROJECT
Planterra Merchandising System
DESIGNERS
Marla Aberegg, Chris Prater,
Roger Pinnick
DESIGN FIRM
Fitch RichardsonSmith
CLIENT/MFR
Weathashade Corporation
AWARD
Bronze 1989

This merchandising solution sets the industry standard for efficient and self-selling product display. Planterra is a family of products combining new indoor plantware containers and a successful line of outdoor plantware developed by Weathashade.

New gondola units provide clear identification of each category of pots. On the packaging, a color information disc at the bottom of each container discusses its features and benefits along with a beauty shot giving ideas for potential uses.

PRODUCT
The Colorcurve® System
DESIGNERS
James Sebastian, John Plunkett,
Frank Nichols, Ralph Stanziola
DESIGN FIRM
Designframe Inc.
CLIENT/MFR
Colorcurve Systems Inc.
AWARD
Gold 1989

The Colorcurve® System is a new color specification product designed to communicate color selections precisely, based on recent technological advances in the industrial manufacture of color. The system consists of two permanent reference atlases, corresponding swatch decks, books and color sheets, a system guide and color-selection tools for specifiers, and a data reference book for manufacturers.

PRODUCT
Color Burst Chip Cosmetic Sample
System
DESIGNERS
Edward L. Paas, Bruce Nelson,
Dave Byram
DESIGN FIRM
3M Company Industrial Design
CLIENT/MFR
3M Consumer Specialty Division
AWARD
Bronze 1989

The Color Burst Chip Cosmetic System is a system for sampling cosmetics in the marketplace. It provides the user with a sample of a product (i.e., lipstick, eye shadow, etc.) that can be tried without fear of contamination from someone who has used it before. The consumer dispenses the chip by placing a finger against the back of the chip and sliding it up and out of the dispenser. The individual sanitary sample may then be tried in the store or taken home for future sampling.

PROJECT
Pixel Paint Professional Packaging
DESIGNERS
Primo Angeli, Mark Crumpacker,
Ray Honda
DESIGN FIRM
Primo Angeli, Inc.
CLIENT/MFR
Supermac Technology
AWARD
Bronze 1990

Pixel Paint Professional is the first software paint program capable of rendering in 32 bit color and released to the consumer market. The design of this package is distinctive, setting the program apart from standard paint programs. The entire package, from concept to mechanical, was designed on a Macintosh using the Pixel Paint Professional.

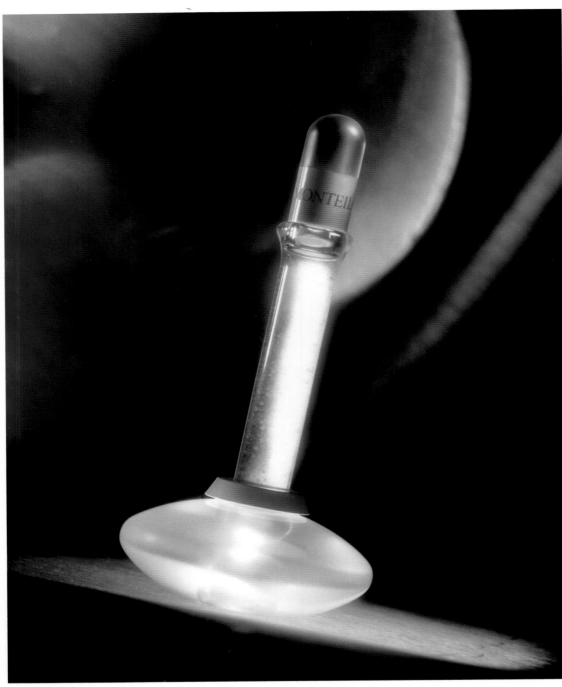

PROJECT
Lightyears Eye Area Formula
DESIGNERS
Kenneth Hirst, Heidi Schwenk
DESIGN FIRM
Cato Gobe Hirst
CLIENT/MFR
Revlon Subsidiary, Germaine Monteil
Cosmetiques, Inc.
AWARD
Silver 1990

This design is inspired by the test tube, the ultimate clinical symbol, and the romance of the French lifestyle. The package holds Germaine Monteil's new "anti-gravity" moisture complex which minimizes the appearance of aging around the eyes. The packaging creates an air of fantasy and magic by combining symbols of advanced technologies with inviting, organic forms.

PROJECT
Veryfine Juice Bottles
DESIGN FIRM
Selame Design Staff
CLIENT/MFR
Veryfine, Inc.
AWARD
Silver 1990

This bottle design strengthens the national brand recognition of Veryfine's line of fruit juices without losing the brand equity and consumer recognition value of the original design created in 1975. It allows the company's name to take center stage and creates a protectable brandmark.

PROJECT
An Open Conversation: Steelcase Corporate Design Center Brochure
DESIGNERS
Kwok C. Chan, Wendie Wulff, Shelley Evenson
DESIGN FIRM
Fitch RichardsonSmith
CLIENT/MFR
Steelcase, Inc.
AWARD
Silver 1990

This piece was designed to announce the opening of the Steelcase Corporate Design Center and its new communication process. The designers created a process that allows the customer to cover layers of information creatively and interestingly. The design and copy are inseparable and express a multi-level story of how communication between all the people involved will produce new kinds of design solutions for Steelcase and its customers.

PROJECT
RISC System/6000 Usability Posters
DESIGNERS
Tristan Merino, Edward Sabella,
Colleen Sweeney
DESIGN FIRM
IBM Austin Design Center
CLIENT/MFR
IBM Corporation
AWARD
Bronze 1990

These posters promote the usability aspects of the RISC System/6000 with a graphic that is informative yet visually interesting. Each poster reveals a different aspect of the product's use. The posters' primary graphic motif is the corner of a computer "window," complete with "pull down" menus, illustrating another aspect of what makes the software for this system easy to use.

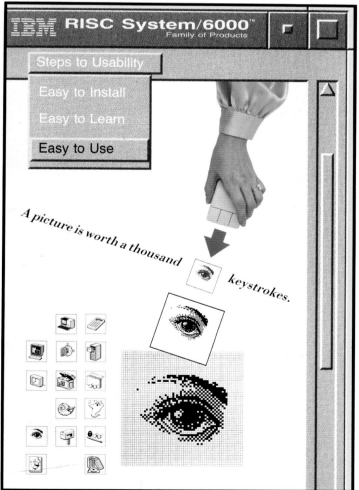

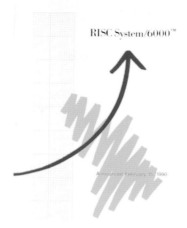

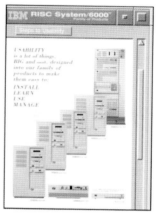

181

MACHINERY AND INDUSTRIAL PRODUCTS

TSP TURRET STOCKPICKER

"Thoughtful treatment of the operator's environment makes this product a winner. The designers achieved their goal of creating a functional and aesthetic workstation for the operator."

—*Juror* **Clyde Foles,** IDSA

PRODUCT
GPW Walkie Pallet Truck
DESIGNERS
Gregory S. Breiding, David B. Smith
DESIGN FIRM
Fitch RichardsonSmith
CLIENT/MFR
Crown Equipment Co.
AWARD
Bronze 1989

This compact, battery-powered lift truck is designed for use on loading docks and can haul up to 4,000 pounds of palletted goods to staging or storage locations. It is also small enough to work within a re- tail environment stocking shelves. The design features a slanted, recessed gauge display and a storage tray with ribbed detail for im- proved traction when the operator stands on top of the truck to reach the second shelf in a warehouse.

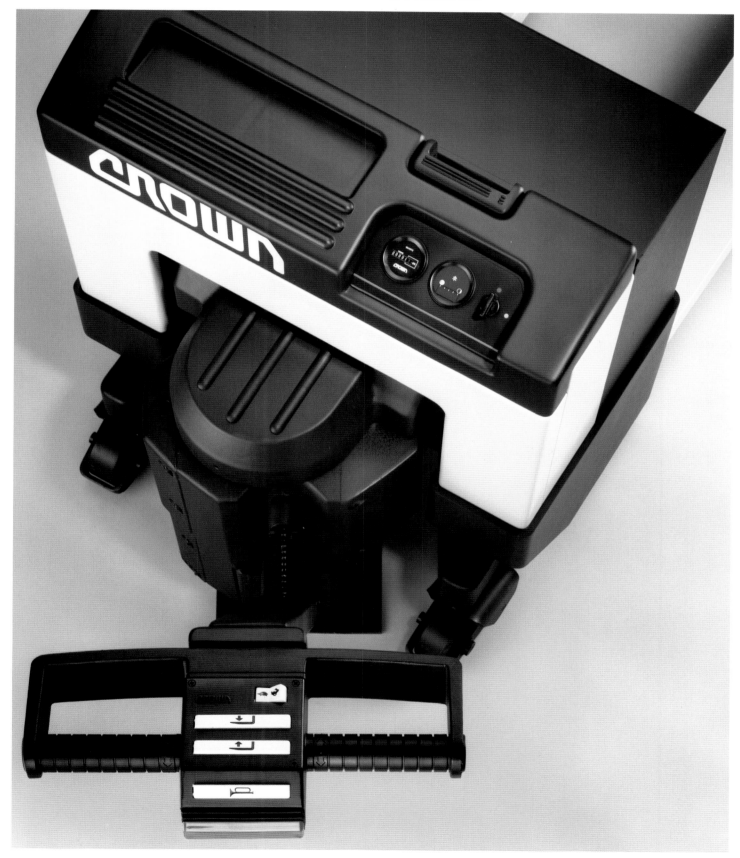

PROJECT
90 Series Maximizer Combine
DESIGNERS
James Conner, William Crookes,
Stephen Miggels, Daniel Nickles
DESIGN FIRM
Henry Dreyfuss Associates
CLIENT/MFR
Deere & Company
AWARD
Bronze 1989

Operator comfort is crucial in this piece of farm machinery which is used over long periods of time during a relatively short period when crops must be harvested quickly and efficiently. The design reconfigured all the operator cab controls so that major controls travel with the operator's suspension seat. Noise levels were significantly reduced in the cab, and belts and chains were reduced by 33 percent.

PRODUCT
7100 Magnum Tractor
DESIGNERS
Gregg C. Montgomery,
Ralph C. Lanphere, et. al.
DESIGN FIRM
Montgomery Design International;
J I Case
CLIENT/MFR
J I Case
AWARD
Gold 1988

A technically superior agricultural tractor, the 7100 Magnum set a new standard in the industry. Its many innovations include: a fully enclosed hood designed to manage airflow, reduce noise and provide safer operation; all plastic body components in both the hood and cab to resist corrosion and reduce weight; a repositioned exhaust stack resulting in unobstructed forward visibility; and dual, radar-controlled LCD readouts that can convey valuable information such as the amount of acreage covered within a specified time frame.

PRODUCT
Dryvac M 100S
DESIGNER
George Teodorescu
DESIGN FIRM
Leyboldesign USA
CLIENT/MFR
Leybold Vacuum Products
AWARD
Bronze 1989

The Dryvac M 100S provides a high-quality, clean vacuum essential in semiconductor processes such as coating, sputtering and crystal growing. The design offers service-friendly product architecture, concentrating all controls, flanges, and connections in a main modular "backbone core" with removable lateral panels.

PRODUCT
TMP 340
DESIGNER
George Teodorescu
DESIGN FIRM
Leyboldesign USA
CLIENT/MFR
Leybold-Inficon Inc.
AWARD
Silver 1990

Used in Silicon wafer coating, CD-manufacturing and scientific applications, the TMP 340 was designed to solve the problems of its predecessor—complex setup and a tangle of wires and tubes around a pump. More compact, it offers a more sensible distribution of connections. The design is also easier and less expensive to manufacture.

PRODUCT
T S P **Turret Stock Picker**
DESIGNERS
Gregory S. Breiding, David B. Smith,
Rainer Teufel
DESIGN FIRM
Fitch RichardsonSmith
CLIENT/MFR
Crown Equipment Co.
AWARD
Gold 1989

A turret-style forklift truck, the TSP is a specialized piece of industrial equipment used to transfer heavy loads and maximize warehouse distribution center space and density. The design is based on studies of the working environment, task analysis and anthropomorphic data for both male and female operators. One of the TSP's many features is a fully adjustable, electrically powered seat that folds up and out of the way, facilitating the operator's movement within the cab when tasks require a standing position.

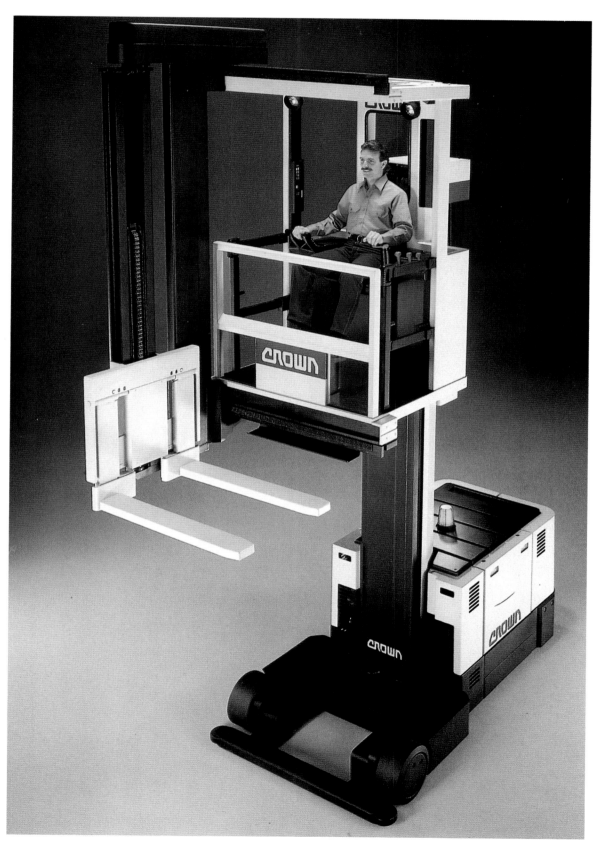

PRODUCT
Power Cooker
DESIGNERS
Rick Wendorf, Stacy Jayne King-Murray
DESIGN FIRM
Lang Manufacturing Company
CLIENT/MFR
Lang Manufacturing Company
AWARD
Bronze 1989

This round-shaped power cooker is controlled by a microprocessor and automatically bakes individual pizzas, eliminating the need for users to make decisions about cooking time variables. The cooking surface rotates which allows the pizza to pass uniformly through the infrared rays, ensuring an evenly baked product. Designed for simplicity of operation, the machine can easily be used by an untrained kitchen helper.

PRODUCT
Pac200 Semiconductor Processor
DESIGNER
Khodi Feiz
DESIGN FIRM
Texas Instruments
CLIENT/MFR
Texas Instruments
AWARD
Bronze 1990

The Pac200 is a semiconductor processing machine used in front-end clean rooms for the manufacture of silicon slices. The design cut the cost of manufacturing the exterior house and interior electronic interfaces by 50 percent compared to its predecessor.

PRODUCT
Lightning Die Grinder Line
Redesign Program
DESIGNERS
Robert B. Staubitz, Roy Heinz,
Charles F. T. Merritt
DESIGN FIRM
Group Four Design
CLIENT/MFR
Ingersoll-Rand Company
AWARD
Bronze 1989

The Lightning Die Grinder
Line is a modular family of
128 pneumatic die grinders
used in every type of manufacturing industry to remove
and finish a variety of parts
and surfaces. Its advanced
ergonomic design provides
optimal operator comfort
while lowering noise, de-
creasing thermal transfers
and reducing vibration for
quiet, smooth operation.

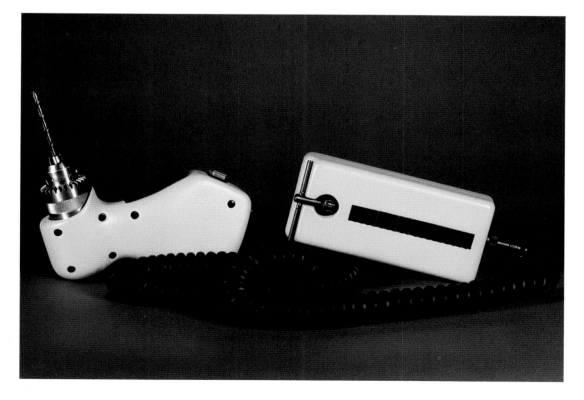

PRODUCT
Drill/Driver
DESIGNER
Jon Taylor while a student at the
University of Kansas
AWARD
Bronze 1989

This tool, intended for the
commercial market, is de-
signed to accommodate drill-
ing or screwing in tight
spaces. The drill unit is
pared down to the least
number of parts needed to
perform the operation, with
all other parts located in the
power pack, including bat-
teries, chuck key holder, circuit breaker and torque
control circuitry. The power
pack can be belt-clipped or
placed elsewhere at the
user's discretion.

PRODUCT
Lokring Tool
DESIGNERS
Nicholas Talesfore, John Durkin,
David Sinclair
DESIGN FIRM
Talesford Design & Engineering
CLIENT/MFR
Lokring Corp.
AWARD
Silver 1989

This hand tool line uses hydraulic pressure to squeeze a coupling called a lokring, an alternative to costly welding. Safety was a main consideration because of the loading forces (in excess of 20,000 pounds). Because the weight factor was also critical, the designers developed a safety door that performs two functions: it shields fingers from the moving jaw and retains and aligns the lokring axis to the moving jaw axis.

PRODUCT
Estimator
DESIGNER
Ted Ciccone
DESIGN FIRM
Stanley Tools, Division of the
Stanley Works
CLIENT/MFR
Stanley Tools, Division of the
Stanley Works
AWARD
Silver 1988

The Estimator measures lin-
ear distances from two to 30
feet by transmitting inaud-
ible sound waves and calcu-
lating the time it takes the
echo to return. It is operated
by holding the unit flat
against a surface or wall,
momentarily pressing the
side buttons, and then waiting for an audible sound that
signals the completed calcu-
lation. The Estimator is designed to provide ease of
use for both left and right-
handed consumers.

PRODUCT
Rotare Professional Camcorder
DESIGNER
Ronald S. Boeder
DESIGN FIRM
Ampex Corporate Industrial Design
CLIENT/MFR
Ampex Corporation
AWARD
Bronze 1989

A durable, compact, versatile and ergonomically excellent video camera, the Rotare is intended for professional electronic news gathering. It can be used either handheld or on a tripod. Rotare is the only professional camera with a unique central pivot allowing infinite adjustment of elements, including right or left-handed operation.

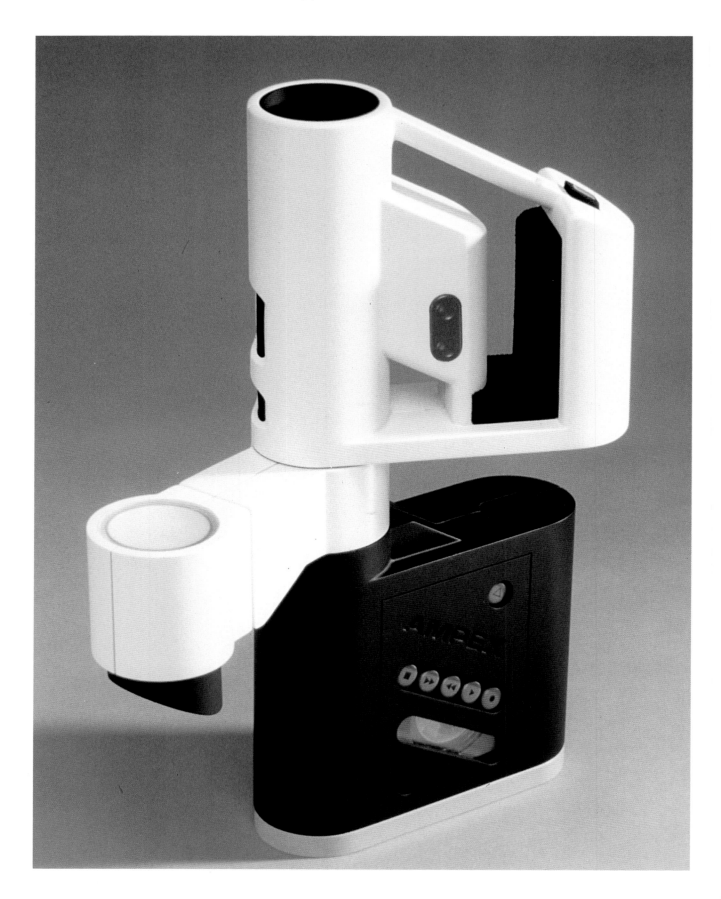

PRODUCT
Exposure Display System Cases
DESIGNERS
Stuart Karten, John Trengove,
Don Jeffries
DESIGN FIRM
Stuart Karten Design
CLIENT/MFR
Exposure Displays Systems, Inc.
AWARD
Silver 1989

These cases were designed
specifically to transport the
components of the Exposure
Display System. The cases'
angled sides allow the
30″ × 96″ panels to roll up
neatly. Designed for durability, the cases can be
checked as airline baggage or
shipped via UPS. The cases
have interlocking lugs so
that two units can be
strapped and wheeled
together.

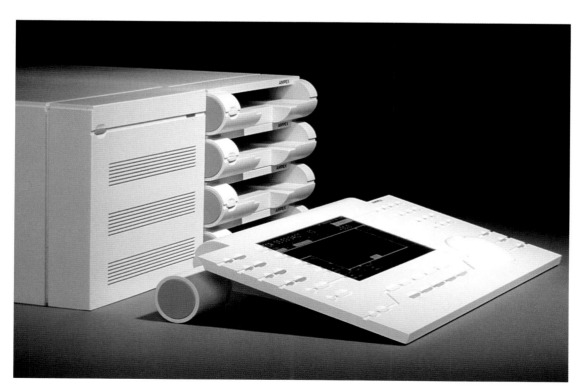

PRODUCT
Modular Professional Video
Recorder System
DESIGNER
Ron Boeder
DESIGN FIRM
Ampex Corporate Industrial Design
CLIENT/MFR
Ampex Corporation
AWARD
Bronze 1989

This video recorder system
is intended for professional
recording, editing and broad-
casting in a studio environment. From one to four
transports are available for
dubbing and editing, and all
controls are on a single control panel/keyboard. Its modularity, expandability and
condensed controls make
this a truly revolutionary
recorder system.

CHAPTER 9

MEDICAL AND SCIENTIFIC PRODUCTS

ATFS SURGICAL FOOTSWITCH

"What I find most appealing about this product is that the solutions to the ergonomic and manufacturing issues are responsible for the interesting visual solution!"

—*Juror* **Barbara Lewis,** IDSA

NUCLEUS BLOOD ANALYZER

"The whole design maintains a strong technological rationalism while being immediately accessible and unthreatening to the user."

—*Jury Chair* **Gianfranco Zaccai,** IDSA

550 EXPRESS ANALYZER

"This product vividly shows the importance of carefully analyzing each step of the design process, from human factors to manufacturing and service."

—*Jury Chair* **Charles Pelly,** IDSA

PRODUCT
ATFS Surgical Footswitch
DESIGNER
Allan Cameron
DESIGN FIRM
S. G. Hauser Associates, Inc.
CLIENT/MFR
Alcon Surgical Instruments
AWARD
Gold 1989

The footswitch is a universal control for the handpiece used by surgeons in several fields of eye surgery. Placed under the operating table, it cannot be seen by the surgeon. The distinctive, graphically stated form of the ATFS Surgical Footswitch adds to the surgeon's ability to spatially relate to the footpedal without actually seeing it.

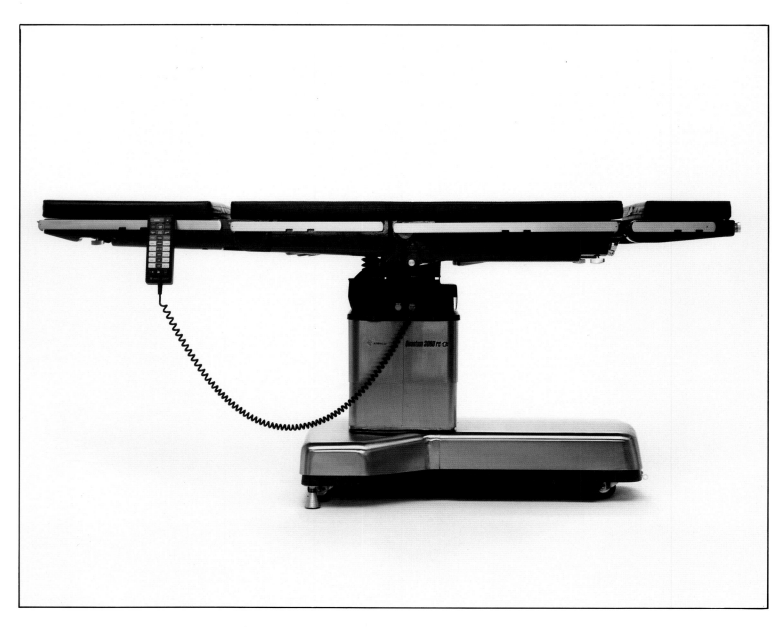

PRODUCT
Quantum 3080 RC General Surgery
Table
DESIGNER
Ward L. Sanders
DESIGN FIRM
AMSCO
CLIENT/MFR
AMSCO
AWARD
Silver 1989

This table's design is based on extensive human factors analysis of patient positioning dynamics, surgical team interface, control and interaction with ancillary equipment. The design provides patients with safety and comfort: anesthesiologists with a logical, easy to use and reliable control system: and the surgical team and their equipment with unimpaired access to the patient and operative site.

PRODUCT
Gilbaugh Aspirator
DESIGNERS
Scott Rowley, Jack Snoke; Joseph Genese of C. R. Bard
DESIGN FIRM
inno
CLIENT/MFR
C. R. Bard, Inc.
AWARD
Bronze 1990

This disposable medical instrument allows physicians to easily and safely obtain prostate gland tissue samples on an outpatient basis. The design uses a pistol grip configuration that promotes single-handed operation, precise and detailed control, reduced physician/user fatigue and ease of sample ejection.

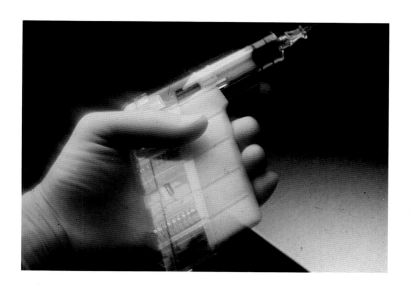

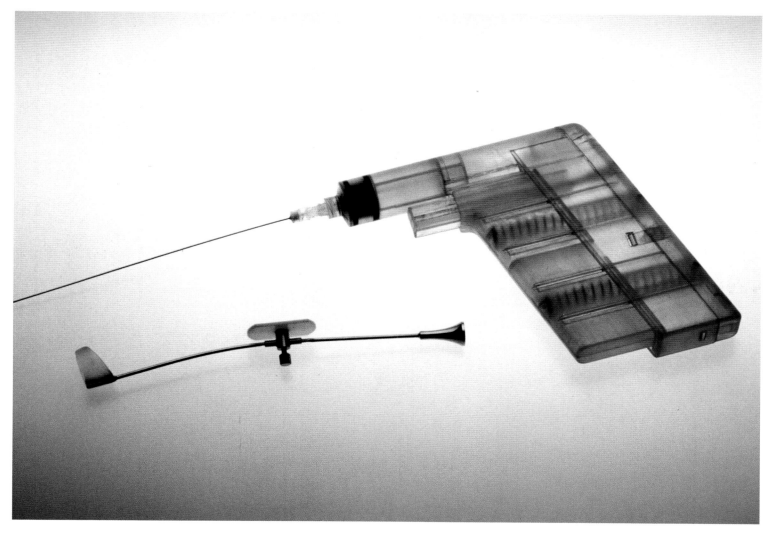

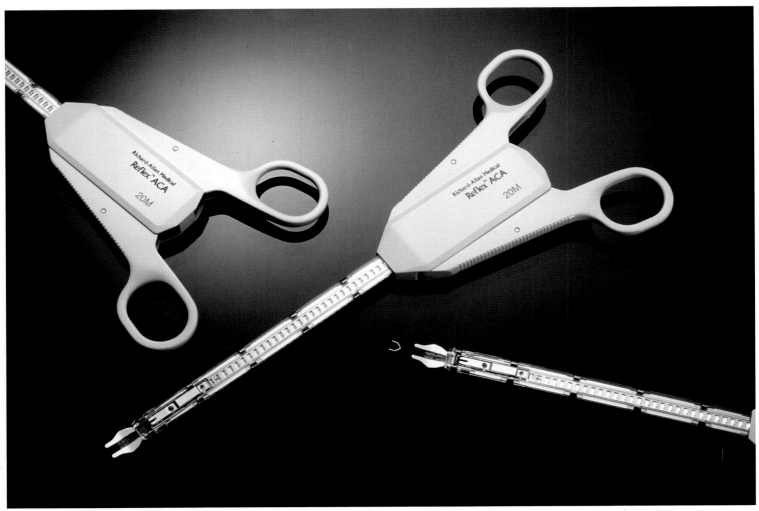

PRODUCT
Reflex ACA
DESIGNERS
Paul Mulhauser, Chris Brooks, Douglas Spranger
DESIGN FIRM
Human Factors/Industrial Design, Inc.
CLIENT/MFR
Richard-Allan Medical
AWARD
Bronze 1989

The Reflex ACA is a disposable, multiple-use surgical automatic clip applier instrument that replaces single-shot, reusable devices that must be manually loaded for each clip and sterilized for each surgery.

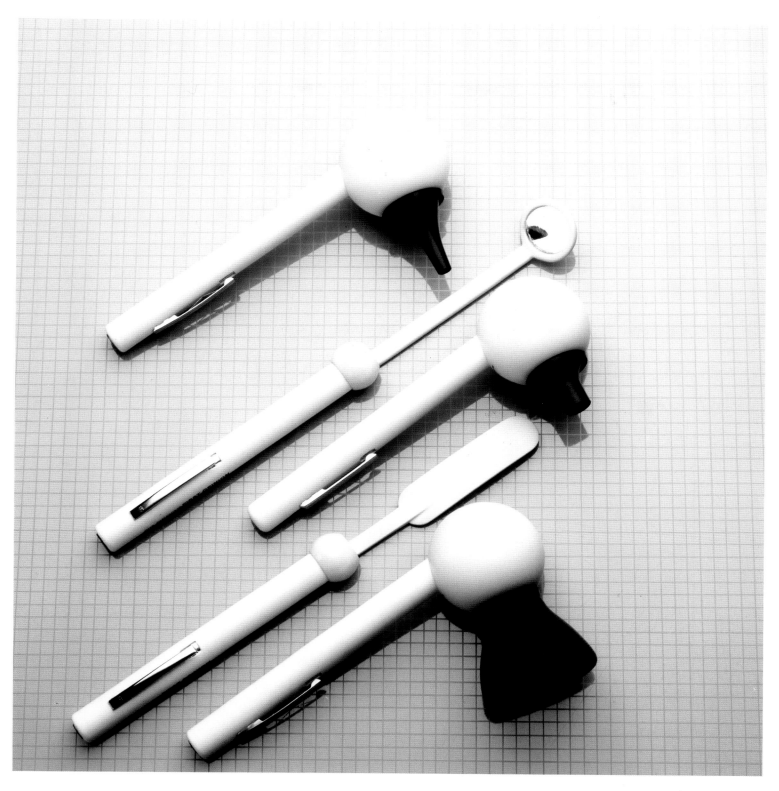

PRODUCT
Dr. Dedo's First Opinion Earlight
DESIGNER
Douglas J. Medema
DESIGN FIRM
Creative Works, Inc.
CLIENT/MFR
PANEX Corporation
AWARD
Silver 1988

The Earlight enables individuals to monitor ear problems in the home and to communicate better with their doctor. It is simple and durable in construction, inexpensive to manufacture, unintimidating in appearance, and ergonomically correct.

PRODUCT
Organ Transporter
DESIGNERS
LeRoy J. LaCelle, Tony Grasso, Paul Ferner
DESIGN FIRM
Designhaus, Inc.
AWARD
Bronze 1989

The Organ Transporter is a total, mobile organ life support device for two to four human organs. The innovation in the design is the organization and position format of the product's components. All major weight devices are in a horizontal base, and all major user interface requirements are in a vertical tower.

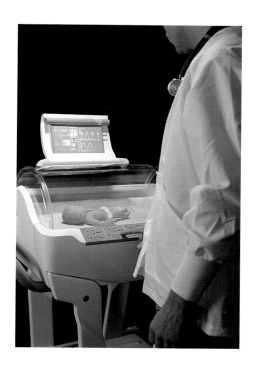

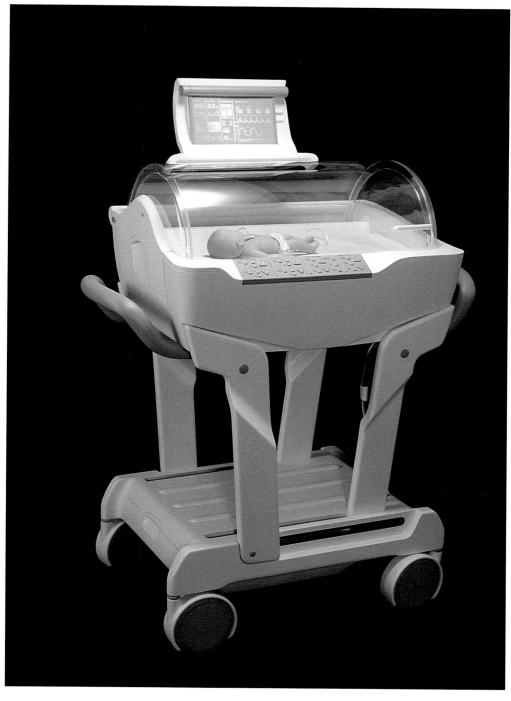

PRODUCT
Doma Neonatal Transport Isolate
DESIGNER
Tigh Mackenzie Belden while a
student at the University of Illinois
DESIGN FIRM
TMB Design
AWARD
Bronze 1990

Doma is a neonatal transport isolate which would provide life support for premature infants during transport between health care facilities. It focuses the operator's interaction on the infant by integrating the separate life support systems through a micro-processor controlled interface. The softer form vocabulary is an alternative to more threatening and inappropriate designs.

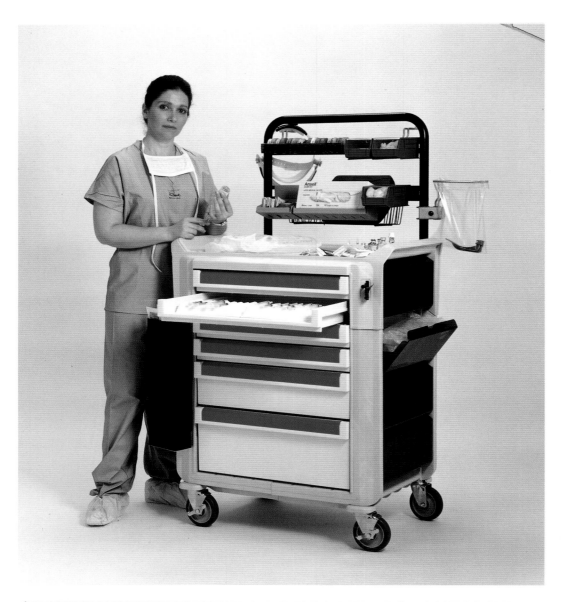

PRODUCT
MetroFlex Specialized Hospital Carts
DESIGNER
Robert J. Welch
DESIGN FIRM
InterMetro Industries Corporation
CLIENT/MFR
InterMetro Industries Corporation
AWARD
Bronze 1989

The MetroFlex closed cart system offers a workstation approach to meeting specialists' needs. Flexible drawer divider kits, tilt-out bins, handing accessories and label strips put every vital supply where it can be seen, identified and accessed immediately.

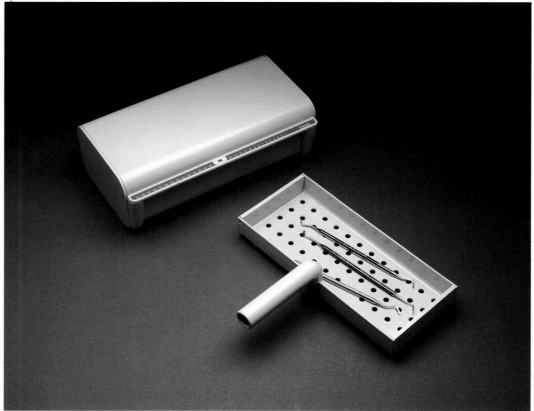

PRODUCT
Pascal Sterilizing/Disinfecting Tray
DESIGNERS
Frank Hosick, Larry Smith
DESIGN FIRM
Frank Hosick Design
CLIENT/MFR
Pascal, Inc
AWARD
Bronze 1989

Designed for dental offices, the Pascal Tray eliminates touching sterilized instruments. With the instrument tray in place, closing the lid "automatically" lowers it into the disinfecting solution. Instruments are removed by touching the end of the tray on a sterile surface which releases the end door allowing the instruments to slide out without being touched.

PRODUCT
Patient Positioning System (PPS)
DESIGNERS
Victor Cheung, Amy Potts, Matthew Haggerty
DESIGN FIRM
Product Genesis, Inc.
CLIENT/MFR
Massachusetts General Hospital
AWARD
Bronze 1990

The purpose of the PPS is to position patients in the path of a proton beam targeted on a tumor to break down the bad tissue while leaving surrounding health tissue intact. The overall form of the PPS is designed to emphasize the importance of accuracy and function, while communicating friendliness to the patient and operator.

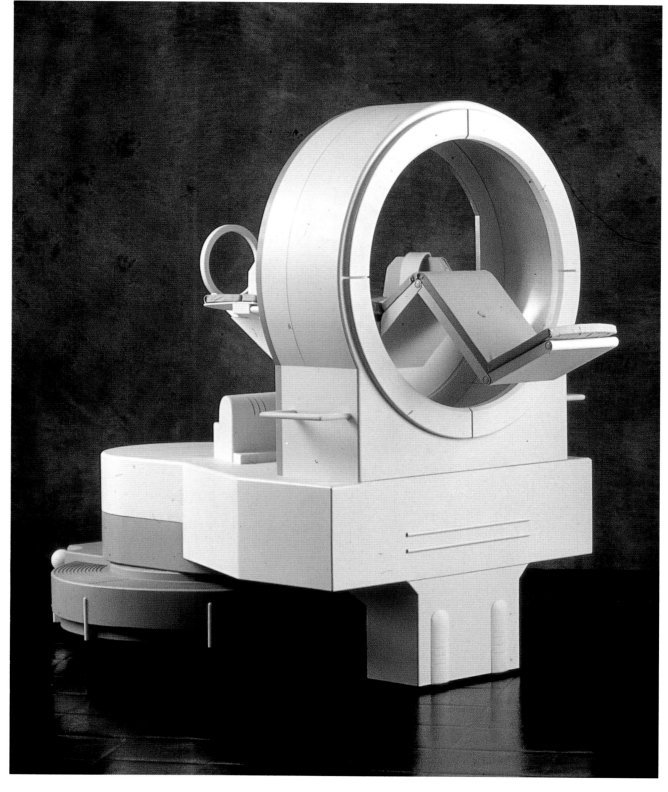

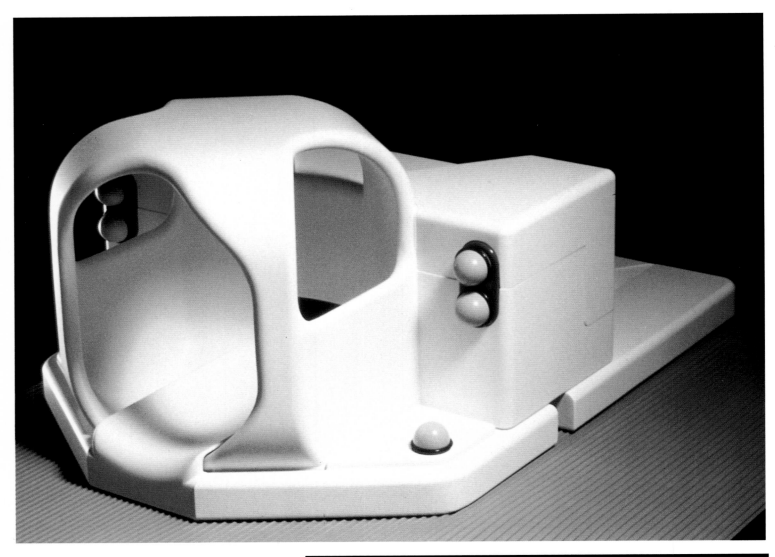

PRODUCT
Vertical Field Quadrature (VFQ)
DESIGNERS
John Amber, Stephen Albert,
John Hoving
DESIGN FIRM
GVO, Inc.
CLIENT/MFR
Resonex, Inc.
AWARD
Silver 1989

An accessory headcoil for
magnetic resonance imaging
systems, the VFQ is designed
to facilitate the patient's
entry and exit into the head-
coils. Large visual passage-
ways help minimize the
claustrophobic aspects of
enclosing the head.

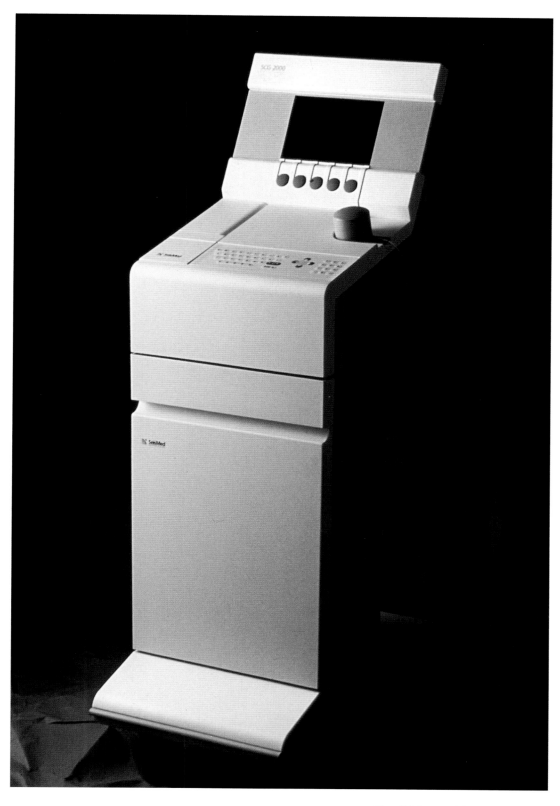

PRODUCT
SCG-2000 Seismocardiograph
DESIGNERS
Eric Mueller, Eugene Reshanov,
Dan Cunagin
DESIGN FIRM
Polivka Logan Designers, Inc.
CLIENT/MFR
SeisMed Instruments, Inc.
AWARD
Bronze 1990

The SCG provides verification to the ECG stress test which allows the physician to measure the heart's efficiency as accurately as possible. The design provides optimum human interface between the technician and the instrument. Only 5 function keys, located directly beneath the screen, are accented, making the SCG easier to use.

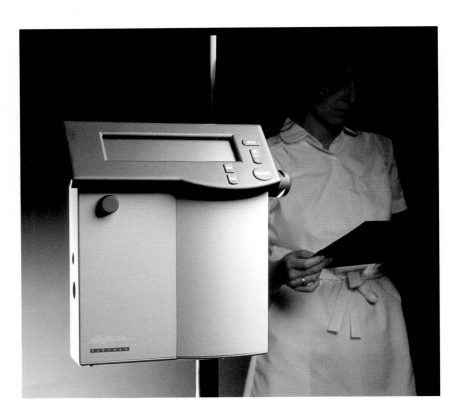

PRODUCT
Arteria
DESIGNERS
Tim Parsey, Peter Spreenberg
DESIGN FIRM
ID TWO
CLIENT/MFR
Paramed
AWARD
Silver 1989

A non-invasive diagnostic device, Arteria monitors blood pressure continuously without the need to insert a catheter into an artery. The overall product form minimizes Arteria's height, keeping its use of vertical space on the IV pole to a minimum.

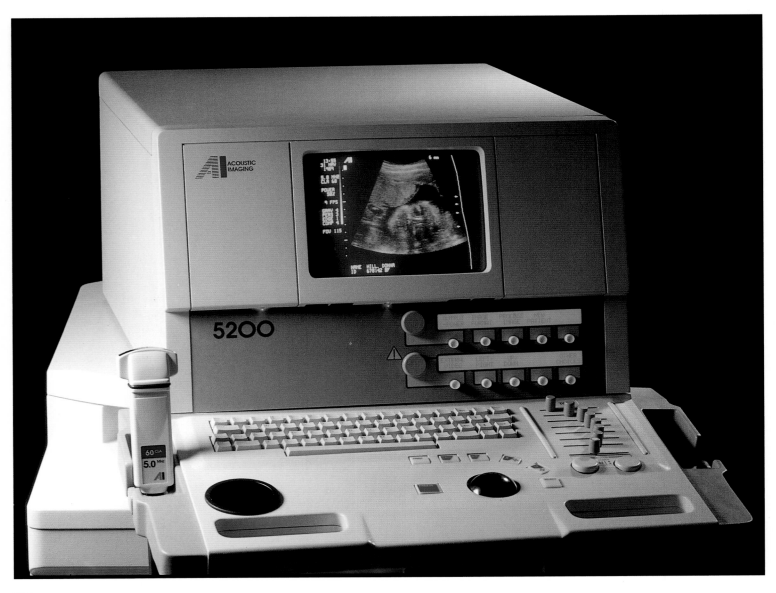

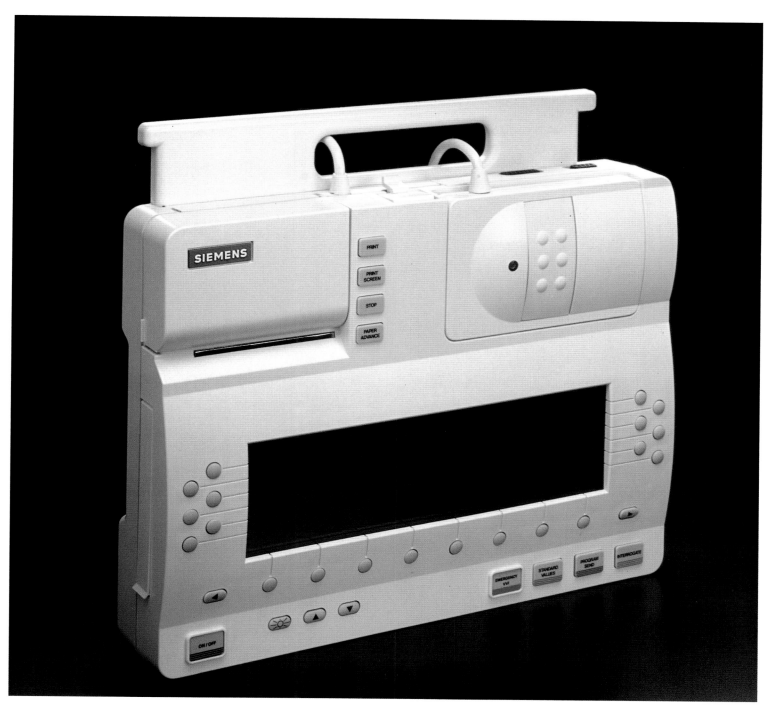

PRODUCT
AI5200 Ultrasound Scanner System
DESIGNER
Roy Fischer, now with Designology
DESIGN FIRM
Fischerdesign, Inc.
CLIENT/MFR
Acoustic Imaging
AWARD
Silver 1989

The AI5200 is a full-feature, high-resolution, mobile ultrasound scanner used by trained medical personnel. User friendly hard and software enable single-handed operation of all controls while scanning with the selected transducer. Successful scan images are the result of a harmonious integration of machine performance and operator skill.

PRODUCT
Universal Programmer—Model 3060
DESIGNERS
David Hines, Kevin Clay, Mark Andersen
DESIGN FIRM
Bartlett Design Associates, Inc.
CLIENT/MFR
Siemens-Pacesetter Systems
AWARD
Bronze 1990

Through a small, handheld telemetry device held against the patient's chest, the Universal Programmer is used to program pacemaker's to specific heart rates and to transmit diagnostic information. The design features overall proportion and organization within a functional yet non-rigid form.

PRODUCT
DI Analytical Balance
DESIGNERS
Sohrab Vossoughi, Henry Chin,
Dave Knaub
DESIGN FIRM
ZIBA Design
CLIENT/MFR
Denver Instruments
AWARD
Bronze 1990

The DI Analytical Balance is a laboratory scale used for highly accurate weight measurements. While the design conveys an image of technological sophistication, the DI Analytical Balance is easy to operate, using a "one key, one function" approach.

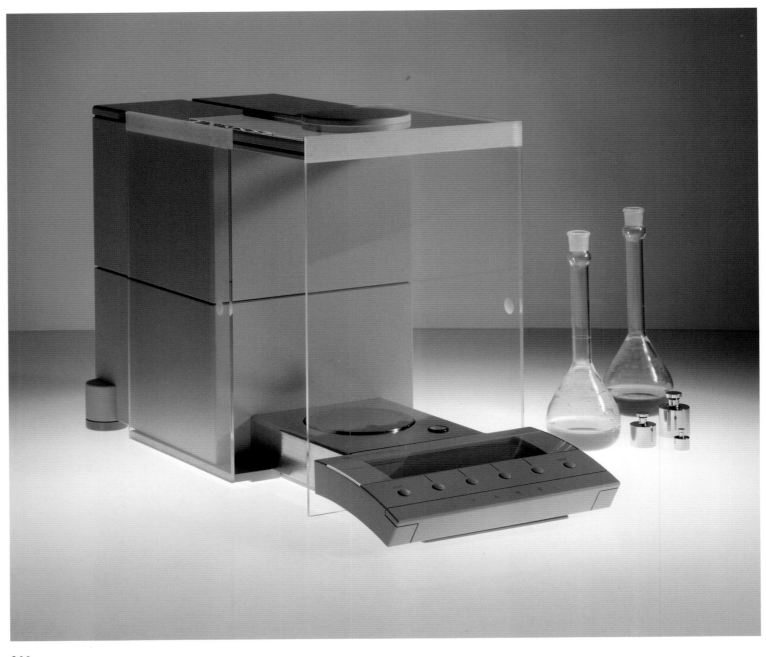

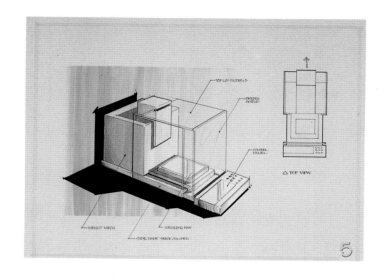

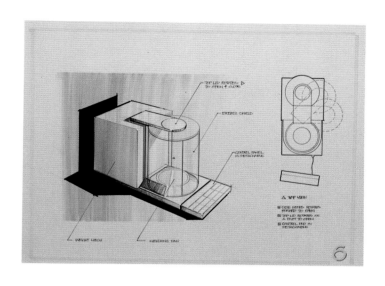

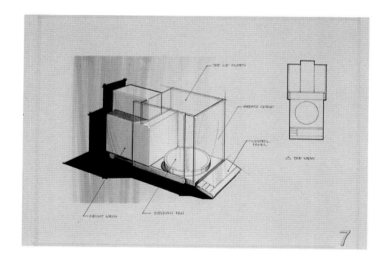

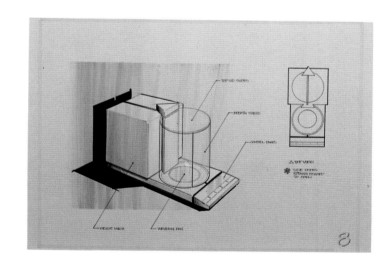

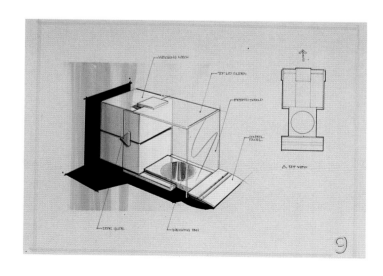

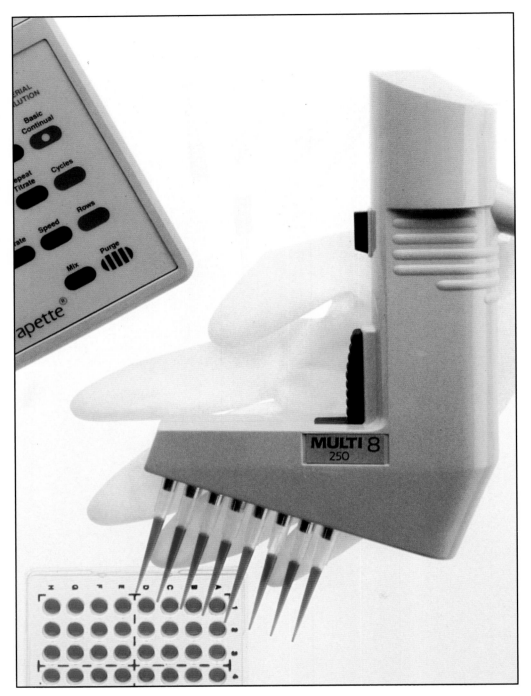

PRODUCT
MULTI-CHANNEL Pipettor
DESIGNERS
Matthew Bantly, Jack R. Harkins
DESIGN FIRM
Roche Harkins Inc.
CLIENT/MFR
Matrix Technologies
AWARD
Bronze 1989

Multi-channel pipettes re used in high-volume labs to enable technicians to simultaneously fill all the wells in a row of a cell-plate. The MULTI-CHANNEL is unique in that all of the functions are inputted into the console which is connected by a cable to the handset. The user only has to press the trigger on the handset to complete the inputted function.

PRODUCT
Computing Densitometer
DESIGNERS
Jeff Smith, Robert Brunner, Braxton
Lathrop, Gerard Furbershaw
DESIGN FIRM
Lunar Design
CLIENT/MFR
Molecular Dynamics
AWARD
Silver 1988

The Computing Densitometer
is a laboratory laser scanning instrument used by scientists, researchers and
technicians. Designed to
minimize apparent and ac-
tual size, the unit fits within
space-constrained installa-
tions and is easy to use at
desk and work heights.

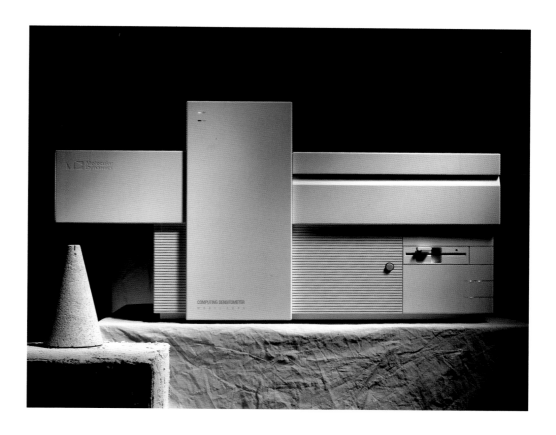

PRODUCT
Microphore 1000, Capillary
Electrophoresis Instrument
DESIGNER
Colin B. Kennedy
DESIGN FIRM
Kennedy Design
CLIENT/MFR
Microphoretic Systems, Inc.
AWARD
Bronze 1989

This instrument performs electrophoresis in a flexible capillary tube, a technique used to separate specific molecules from complex mixtures. The design provides a sturdy enclosure for a sensitive apparatus. Visually, the sine wave shape of the front cover standing against the ruled background suggests the graphical results of the analysis as displayed on the computer monitor.

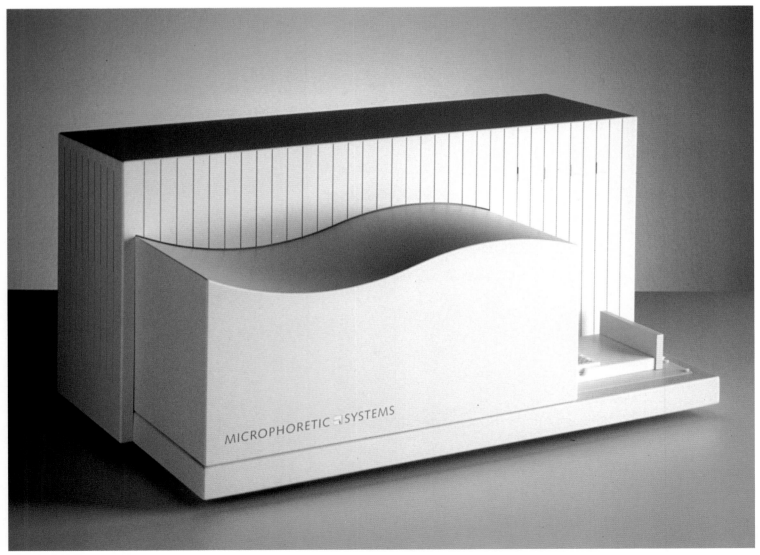

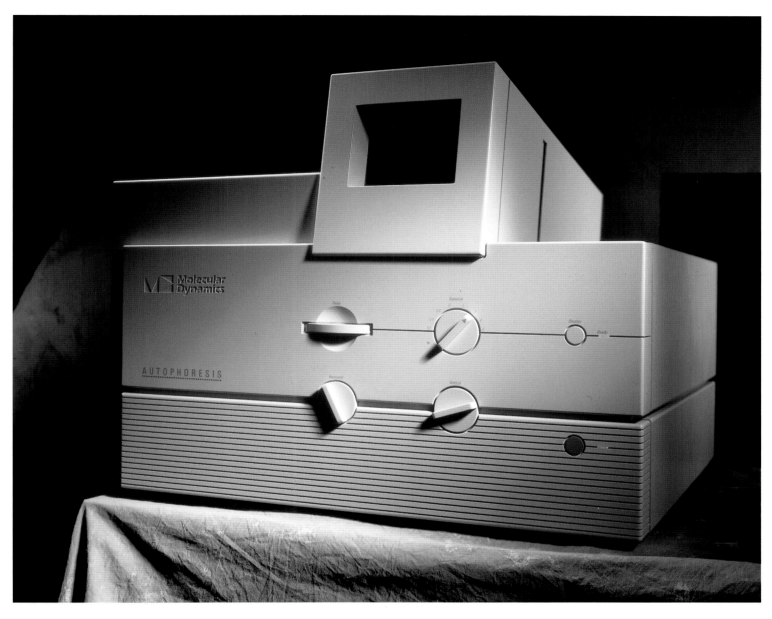

PRODUCT
Autophoresis 1000A
DESIGNERS
Jeff Smith, Robert Brunner
DESIGN FIRM
Lunar Design
CLIENT/MFR
Molecular Dynamics
AWARD
Bronze 1989

The design for this electro-
phoretic gel imaging instrument emphasizes economy
of size, ergonomics and cost
effectiveness. The strategic
use of one molded part on
the front greatly enhances
appearance and accommo-
dates logotype, view port
and controls.

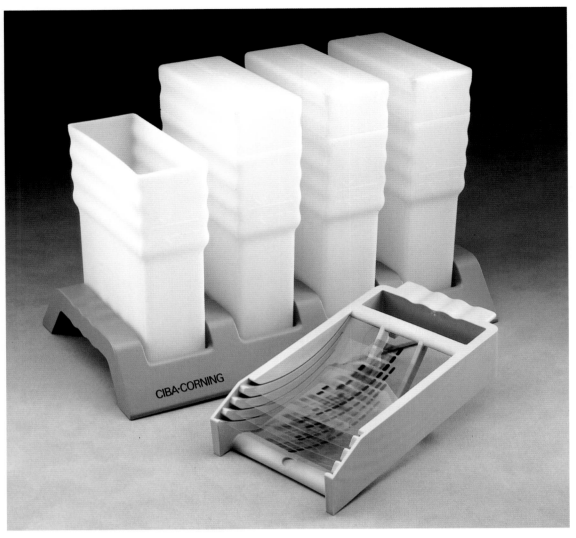

PRODUCT
Universal Gel Processor
DESIGNERS
Dan Gratiot, Ciba Corning
Diagnostics; Jack Harkins,
Roche Harkins
DESIGN FIRM
Roche Harkins
CLIENT/MFR
Ciba Corning Diagnostics Corp.
AWARD
Silver 1990

The Universal Gel Processor is part of a medical diagnostic system used for electrophoresis testing in laboratories by skilled technicians. Ease-of-use was the primary design goal. Moreover, by allowing four gels to be stained simultaneously, the design streamlines the process while better protecting the gels from damage.

PRODUCT
Check-mate Systems
DESIGNERS
Scott Mathis, David Newbold
DESIGN FIRM
Ciba Corning Diagnostics Limited
CLIENT/MFR
Science Products Division, Corning
Glass Works
AWARD
Silver 1989

A hand-held environmental/process system, Check-mate integrates several measurement technologies into a common product architecture. It presents many pieces of simultaneous measurement data to the user in a clear and ordered manner. Rugged and weatherproof, Check-mate can be used outdoors with confidence.

PRODUCT
Nova Nucleus Blood Analyzer
DESIGNERS
Jim Pagella, Richard Randell, Gregory
Kenny, Ben White
DESIGN FIRM
Gregory Fossella Design/A
McCalla/Lackey Company
CLIENT/MFR
Nova Biomedical
AWARD
Gold 1990

Nova is a high-volume, test-selective analyzer used in clinical laboratories. The instrument's many subsystems, including the sample tray and cups, were designed to make this complex system easy for technicians to program, operate and troubleshoot.

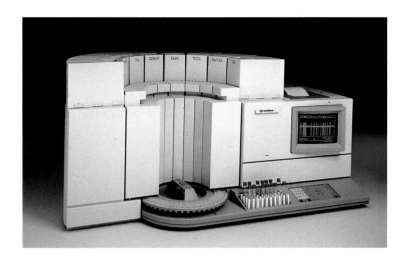

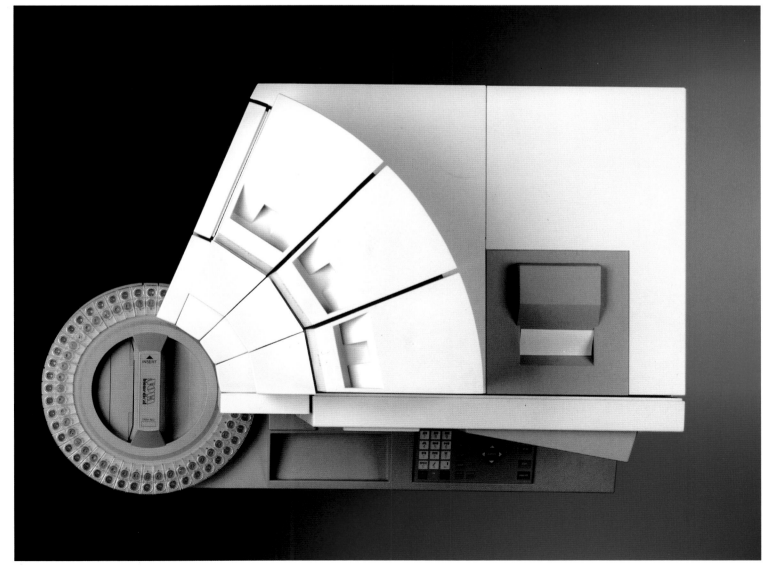

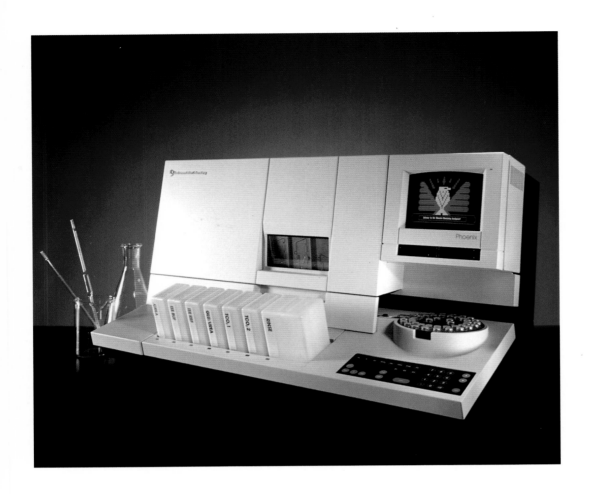

PRODUCT
Phoenix Chemistry/Electrolyte
Analyzer
DESIGNERS
Philip Swift, Stephen Guerrera,
Elizabeth Goodrich
DESIGN FIRM
Design Continuum, Inc.
CLIENT/MFR
Instrumentation Laboratory
AWARD
Silver 1988

A bench-top instrument used
to perform routine blood
tests, the Phoenix is de-
signed to elicit error-free operation by both technical
and non-technical operators.
The image of the product
conveys crisp, clean efficiency as well as the design's
innovative user friendliness.

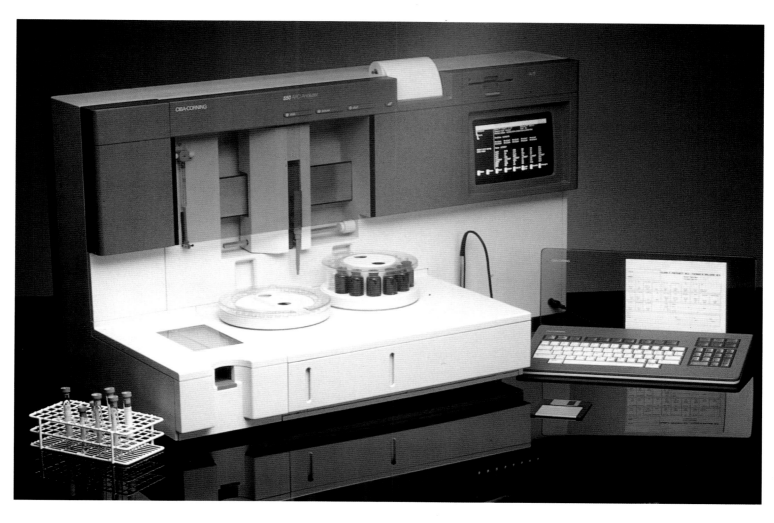

PRODUCT
550 Express Chemistry Analyzer
DESIGNERS
James Couch, Peter Koloski, Elizabeth
B.-N. Sanders
DESIGN FIRM
RichardsonSmith, Inc.
CLIENT/MFR
Ciba Corning Diagnostics
AWARD
Gold 1988

The 550 Express is a Chemistry Analyzer aimed at low to medium volume laboratories. Designed in an "L-shaped" configuration, the Express is easy to use, understand, maintain and service. It reflects good, straightforward organization of components based on users' task sequences and laboratory expectations.

PRODUCT
"A" Series Meter Line
DESIGNERS
Tom Paquette, Laura Brockway, Paul
Sydlowski
DESIGN FIRM
Orion Research, Inc.
CLIENT/MFR
Orion Research, Inc.
AWARD
Bronze 1990

These meters measure low concentration levels of pH, sodium, ammonia and other chemicals in samples of water, food, beverages, paint, etc. Used at both field and laboratory sites, the "A" Series Meter Line is easy to clean and offers simple, menu-driven software.

DESIGNS FOR THE FUTURE

SATELLITE ANTENNA

"This design exploration illustrates that it is possible, through sensitive design, to tame a technological artifact which often litters the landscape of America."

—*Juror* **Bill Moggridge**, IDSA

GOBI CAR/TRUCK

"The Gobi challenges our notion that a 'truck' must be macho and succeeds in being visually acceptable to a wider range of buyers."

—*Juror* **Martin Smith** IDSA

THE ELECTRONIC PLANE

"This concept shows imagination and forward thinking and is executed impeccably with a strong aesthetic presence."

—*Juror* **Bill Moggridge**, IDSA

SEIKO COLOR LCD MONITOR

"This product is stimulating and dynamic from any perspective with details executed to create a high level of harmony and excitement."

—*Juror* **Jack Beduhn**, IDSA

PRODUCT
BioScan
DESIGNERS
Thomas Dempsey and Clay Johnson
while students at Auburn University
AWARD
Gold 1989

The BioScan is a mobile x-ray system that uses digital technology instead of film to record the x-ray. The digital process not only eliminates the need for conventional film and developing, it enables the doctor to see the x-ray immediately on a video screen. Because this system reduces the need for retakes, it also reduces the radiation that patients are exposed to.

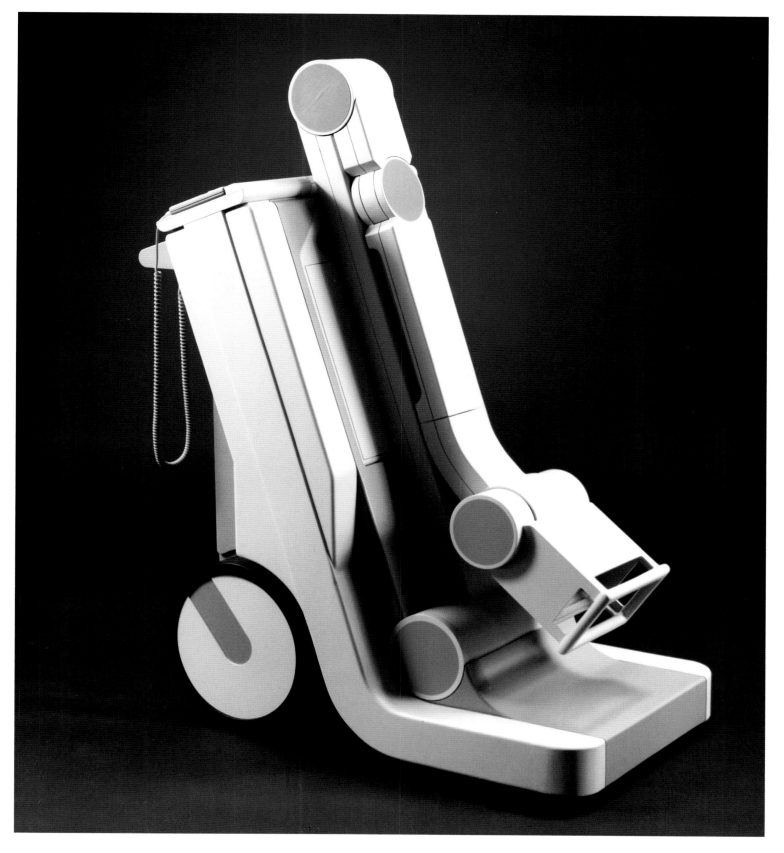

PRODUCT
Paracount Tablet Counter
DESIGNERS
Paul C. Henning,
Matthew K. Haggerty
DESIGN FIRM
Product Genesis Inc.
CLIENT/MFR
Kirby-Lester Electronics
AWARD
Bronze 1989

Paracount is a bench-top tablet counter for the phar-maceutical industry, HMOs and large pharmacies where fast, accurate pill counts are regularly needed. The design presents a clean, medical image in a manner that ex-presses simplicity, perform-ance and ease of use. Paracount disassembles quickly without fastener hardware for easy cleaning of all surfaces in contact with tablets.

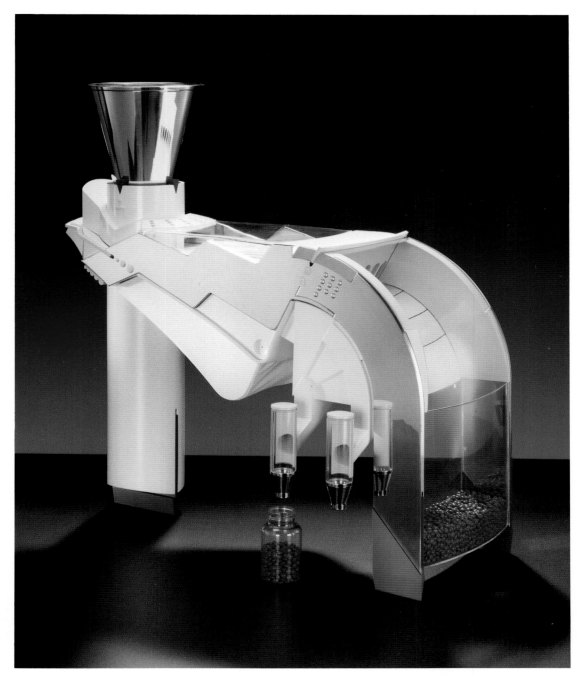

PRODUCT
Critical Care Data Management
DESIGNERS
LeRoy J. LaCelle, Tony Grasso,
Dave Littrell
DESIGN FIRM
Designhaus, Inc.
AWARD
Bronze 1989

Intended for use by hospital intensive care nurses, this interactive wall-mounted dis-play module, with printer and hand-held laser beam controller, provides immedi-ate access to all patient medical records, medication requirements and monitoring data. It also allows operator input of all patient real-time vitals and on-site medical date entries for management of patient care data.

PRODUCT
"Discover" Video Microscope
DESIGNER
John K. Caruso
AWARD
Bronze 1989

Intended for family use, this fully compatible computerized microscope is simple enough for a child to operate, yet sophisticated enough for adult use. The operation is basically the same as a contemporary microscope. The user inserts a prepared slide disc or a live capture specimen tray, adjusts the rotary lens and observes the image on the flat screen LCD. The image can also be recorded and stored on a floppy disc drive.

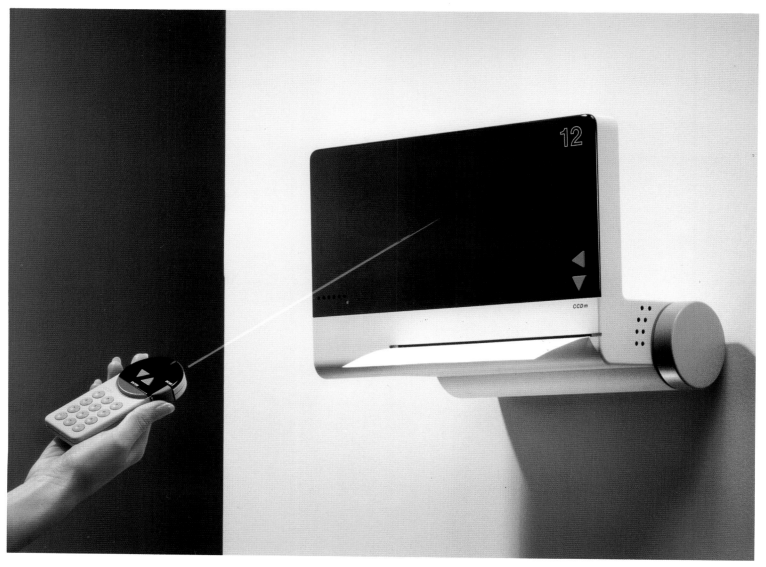

PRODUCT
Satellite Antenna
DESIGNERS
Charles Keane, Steve Monti
DESIGN FIRM
Gregory Fosella Design
CLIENT/MFR
G. E. American Communications
AWARD
Gold 1990

This product is a recommendation for a new generation home roof satellite antenna that dramatically improves the attractiveness and compactness, functionality and operating performance of existing equipment. The result transforms technical and engineering aspects into an elegantly sculptured, highly practical and exceptionally simple statement.

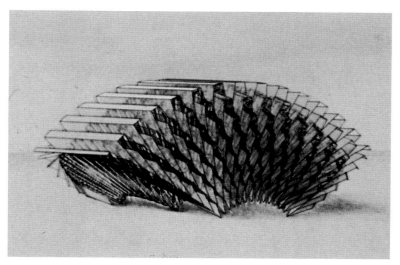

PRODUCT
Radial Expansion Truss System
DESIGNER
Charles Hoberman
AWARD
Silver 1990

The Radial Expansion Truss System adds a new function to structures—the ability to change their size and shape according to changing needs. This is made possible by a unique hybrid structure/mechanism that allows structures to be built up of links connected by pivots that can fold and unfold smoothly and continuously.

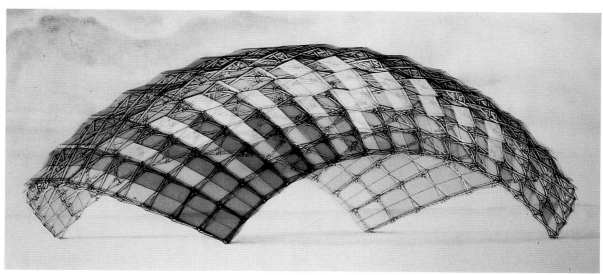

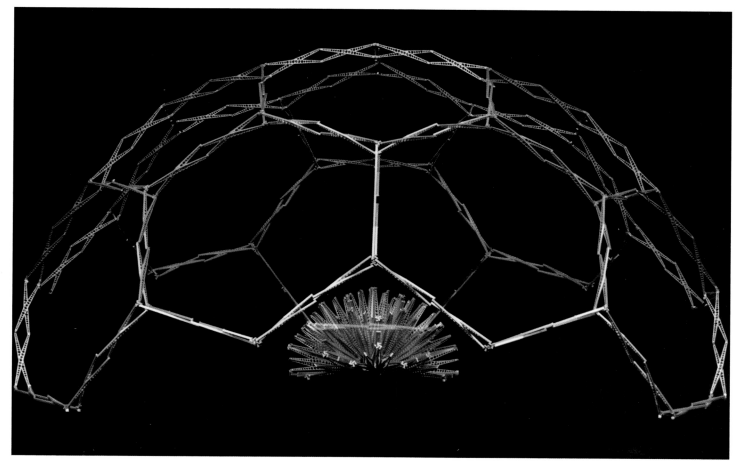

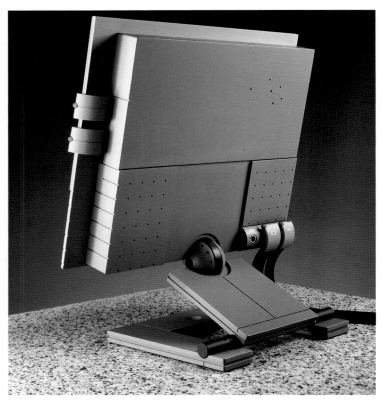

PRODUCT
Seiko Color LCD Monitor
DESIGNER
Edward Cruz
DESIGN FIRM
S. G. Hauser Associates
CLIENT/MFR
Seiko Instruments, Inc.
AWARD
Gold 1989

The design for this conceptual LCD color monitor takes into account the key physical characteristics of LCD technology—compactness, thin profile, small footprint and the possibility for extensive adjustment. The latter is accomplished by a mechanism that combines a sphere and an axle: the axle is the hinge by which the unit raises; the sphere is the means for multi-axis rotation.

PRODUCT
Compuchart
DESIGNER
Ron Boeder
AWARD
Gold 1988

Compuchart is a highly sophisticated computer terminal that stores and retrieves
medical records in a hospital
setting. Tied in with the
mainframe, the terminal can
access information crucial to
diagnosis and treatment.
Compuchart's uniqueness is
its portability: units that
combine the advantages
of the computer and its
database can easily be carried to the patient's room.
Entries can also be made at
remote locations, such as ad-
mitting, laboratories or
radiology.

PRODUCT
Contained Work Environment
DESIGNERS
Scott Graham, Julie Heard,
John Klomp while students at the
Center for Creative Studies
CLIENT/MFR
NCR Corp.
AWARD
Silver 1990

This concept for a workstation divides the workspace
into functional areas such as
physical storage, user interaction and electronic information storage and retrieval.
It features a large format
(24″ × 36″) screen, a background scrim, storage
drawers for disks and files,
two interactive work surfaces,
an adjustable keyboard platform, a moveable footrest, a
task light and a CPU tower.

PRODUCT
Workspace 2000
DESIGNERS
Doug Patton, Joan Ciranny, Rick Jung, Matt Duncan
DESIGN FIRM
Patton Design
CLIENT/MFR
Apple Computer
AWARD
Bronze 1990

The designers of Workspace 2000 were asked by Apple to propose a vision of the future for it to aim toward. They focused their research on their own human needs and tried to create technology scenarios to support them. The result is a fun workplace that can adapt to the user's mood. The traditional desktop products are all modules in the furniture.

PRODUCT
Personal Computer of the Future
DESIGNER
Brian Jablonski while a student intern at NCR Corp.
CLIENT/MFR
NCR Corp.
AWARD
Bronze 1990

The design of this "PC of the future" focuses on the semantic "tower of knowledge," creating a monument to the technology. The design incorporates wireless data transmission techniques which visually simplifies the design and emphasizes technology as an art form.

PRODUCT
Point-of-Sales Terminal
DESIGNERS
Andrew Serbinski, Mario Turchi,
Eric Shank
DESIGN FIRM
Serbinski/MACHINEART
CLIENT/MFR
Fujitsu Ltd.
AWARD
Bronze 1990

The design of this point-of-sales terminal (cash register) is based on research into radical interior and architectural design that sought to understand the avant garde thinking in these fields and extrapolate characteristics that could apply to the design of POS terminals in the mid-1990s.

PRODUCT
Multi-Level Integrated
Computer System
DESIGNERS
Rob Kelley, David Thimm,
Greg Hinzmann
DESIGN FIRM
Center for Creative Studies
CLIENT/MFR
NCR Corporation
AWARD
Gold 1990

This design concept addresses the needs of the executive or professional in the execution of day-to-day activities. It features a multi-level integrated PC system, including a laser printer and a fold-away desk which incorporates an interactive work-surface. A laptop PC nests with the system in facilitating the transfer of data and the recharging of the portable power supply.

PRODUCT
Plymouth Slingshot
DESIGNERS
Craig Durfey, Roger Zrimec
DESIGN FIRM
Chrysler Motors Product Design
CLIENT/MFR
Chrysler Motors
AWARD
Silver 1988

Intended for the youth market of the 1990s, this concept vehicle is designed to be visually exciting, fun to drive, lightweight, affordable and functionally innovative. Blending sports car, motorcycle, and product design, Slingshot's designers generated new approaches to style, function, and manufacturing processes.

PRODUCT
Skylite Convertible Hardtop
DESIGNERS
Bob Patterson, Chad Hines, George Klein
DESIGN FIRM
C&C, Inc.
AWARD
Silver 1990

The Skylite features a glass roof that can be vented like a sunroof, retracted into a targa position, then down into a convertible with no storage or removal required. The top seals like a hardtop. The driver can put the roof into any desired position while driving at highway speeds, a dramatically innovative accomplishment.

PRODUCT
Portofino
DESIGNERS
Dan J. Sims, Joel Baccus,
Kevin Verduyn
DESIGN FIRM
Chrysler Motors Product Design
CLIENT/MFR
Lamborghini/Chrysler Motors
AWARD
Gold 1988

This show car was designed to commemorate Chrysler's purchase of Lamborghini, heralding the return of Chrysler to the European market. Its clean, functional design features four rotational doors, with the two in front pivoting up for ease of entry. The hand-sewn leather interior has an ergonomically adjustable driver's cockpit. Ample space for luggage is provided in both front and rear compartments.

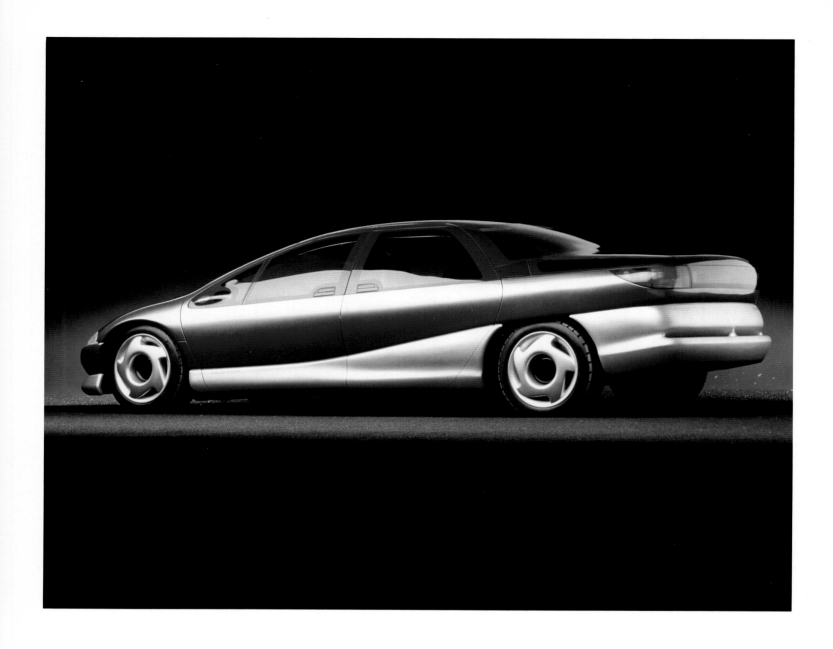

PRODUCT
Millennium
DESIGN FIRM
Chrysler Design Staff
CLIENT/MFR
Chrysler Motors
AWARD
Bronze 1989

The Millennium's clean aerodynamic form conveys Chrysler's direction in car design
for the 1990s. It has large
flush windows with a clear
lower deck panel for en-
hanced rear visibility. The
entire passenger compart-
ment is a structural cocoon
in which the seats, console,
instrument panel and doors
are mechanically integrated
to make up a unified cell.

PRODUCT
GOBI
DESIGNERS
Gerald P. Hirshberg, Bruce Campbell,
Diane Taraskavage, Tom Semple
DESIGN FIRM
Nissan Design International, Inc.
CLIENT/MFR
Nissan Motor Co., Ltd.
AWARD
Gold 1990

Challenging the traditional boundaries of vehicle classi-fication, the Gobi is both an innovative light truck and a spirited two-passenger vehi-cle for everyday use. Its many features include: a he-licopter-like cabin, driver's workstation, flexible pas-senger zone and detachable glove compartment that eas-ily becomes a canvas carry-ing pouch. The truck bed sides are hinged to accom-modate over-sized loads and can also be removed to transform the Gobi into a flatbed truck.

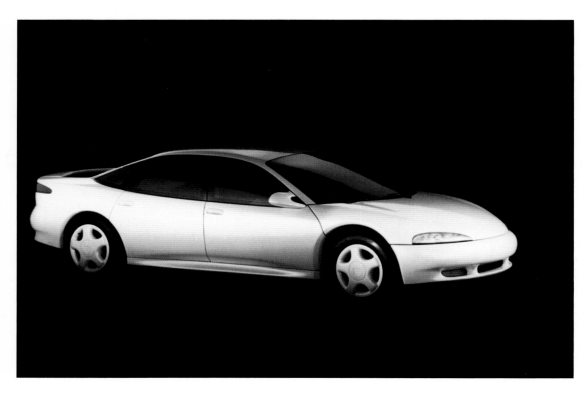

PRODUCT
Eagle Optima Concept Vehicle
DESIGN FIRM
Chrysler Motors Design Staff
CLIENT/MFR
Chrysler Motors–Eagle Marketing
AWARD
Bronze 1990

The Optima's low, sleek appearance is achieved by its cab-forward theme. This theme positions the interior cabin forward on the vehicle's body to allow for a more spacious interior and a low, sporty silhouette. Among the design's advantages to the consumer are optimal driver visibility and maximum interior and cargo compartment space.

PRODUCT
California Concept Camaro
DESIGN FIRM
General Motors Design Staff
CLIENT/MFR
Chevrolet Motor Division
AWARD
Bronze 1989

Designed to appeal to the 2 + 2 sports coupe market in the 1990s and beyond, the California Camaro applies a completely new shape to express the Camaro heritage. It is shorter with a longer wheelbase, providing tighter exterior dimensions and more seating space. The overall design is a continuous development with no corners. Glass is used extensively to lighten the car visually and impart an open feeling to the interior.

PRODUCT
Cadillac Voyage
DESIGN FIRM
General Motors Design Staff
CLIENT/MFR
Cadillac Motor Division
AWARD
Silver 1988

The Cadillac Voyage is a functional test vehicle designed as a "rolling laboratory" to evaluate future Cadillac vehicle concepts. It embodies the elegance, grace and distinctiveness that has been Cadillac's tradition, but also showcases technological advances. One of the world's most aerodynamic gasoline-powered vehicles, the Voyage has a .28 coefficient of drag which contributes dramatically to the car's stability.

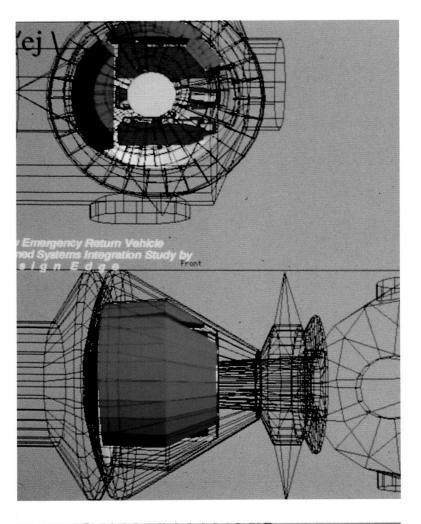

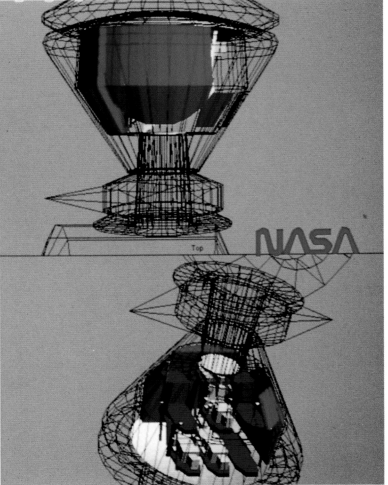

PRODUCT
Crew Emergency Return Vehicle
Man-Systems Study
DESIGNERS
Chipp Walters, Charles Floyd,
Richard Haner
DESIGN FIRM
Design Edge
CLIENT/MFR
NASA/Johnson Space Center
AWARD
Silver 1989

This study defined the crew-member's needs and requirements and proposed design solutions in response. The resulting design allows the crew to enter and leave the vehicle quickly and safely, access control panel areas easily, and manually operate the vehicle. Convenience items, such as waste management, help make the 24–48 hour trip less of an ordeal.

PRODUCT
The Electronic Plane
DESIGNERS
Michael McCoy, Dale Fahnstrom,
David Vandenbranden
DESIGN FIRM
Fahnstrom/McCoy
AWARD
Gold 1990

The electronic plane offers a striking new vision for the future appearance of home entertainment equipment. A dramatic departure from the "Black Box," this design envisions the integration of audio equipment with video data and communications. The design uses the idea of transparency to the user by mounting all the components on a glass plane, 5' × 6', and embedded with a digital bus conductor. Flat color LCD video screens, CD players, speakers, cordless telephones, CCD video cameras and fax/printers can be placed anywhere on the plane and interface with each other.

INDEX

PRODUCTS/PROJECTS

DESIGNERS

DESIGN FIRMS